IMAGES
of America

GAY AND LESBIAN
SAN FRANCISCO

After his visit to the city in 1889, Rudyard Kipling lamented, "San Francisco has only one drawback—'tis hard to leave." Anyone who has enjoyed the great beauty of the city and its attractions certainly would agree.

ON THE COVER: The Castro Street Fair has been a fixture of the LGBT (Lesbian Gay Bisexual and Transgender) calendar since 1974.

IMAGES
of America

GAY AND LESBIAN
SAN FRANCISCO

Dr. William Lipsky

Yours in Pride
Bill Lipsky

ARCADIA
PUBLISHING

Published by Arcadia Publishing
Charleston, South Carolina

Printed in the United States of America

Library of Congress Catalog Card Number: 2006922429

For all general information contact Arcadia Publishing at:
Telephone 843-853-2070
Fax 843-853-0044
E-mail sales@arcadiapublishing.com
For customer service and orders:
Toll-Free 1-888-313-2665

Visit us on the Internet at www.arcadiapublishing.com

For Don Price

It started in 1970 with 30 "hair fairies" marching down Polk Street. The "Unity and More in '84" parade attracted 300,000 people. This year, more than one million will gather to watch the San Francisco Lesbian, Gay, Bisexual, Transgender Pride Celebration.

CONTENTS

ACKNOWLEDGMENTS

Everyone contacted about this project generously gave of their time and expertise. Board of supervisors member Tom Ammiano not only took time out of his extraordinarily crowded schedule to meet but to provide a foreword as well. Terence Kissack, executive director, and Jacob Richards, operations manager of the Gay Lesbian Bisexual Transgender Historical Society of Northern California, cordially provided information, guidance, and patience for all questions and requests, great and small, during the research; Dr. Kissack also agreed to furnish the introduction. Daniel Homsey, director of the Mayor's Office of Neighborhood Services, graciously allowed me to look through his extensive archive of images without restriction or limitation. John D'Alessandro and Peter Gerhauser of the Golden Gate Business Association made all necessary arrangements to use one of the organization's images without individual releases. Richard Marino, of the San Francisco History Center, San Francisco Public Library, found the photograph of Mona Sargent in uncataloged material and brought it to my attention. I am grateful to them all and to their organizations for their enthusiastic assistance.

Images by the following photographers are in the collection of the Gay Lesbian Bisexual Transgender Historical Society of Northern California: Tommi Avocolli-Mecca, page 121 bottom; Crawford Barton, front cover, pages 2, 83 top, 84 bottom, 85 bottom, 88, 93 bottom, and 111 bottom; Alan Bistry, page 81 bottom; Henry Leleu, pages 68 top, 69 top left and right, 74 top, 83 bottom, 85 top, 90, and 95 bottom; Robert Pruzan, pages 74 bottom, 81 top, 97 bottom, 99 top, 100 bottom, 102 top, 110 top and bottom, 112 bottom, 114 bottom, and 115 top and bottom; and Efrin Ramirez, pages 94 bottom left, 101 top, 103 bottom, and 109 top; Marie Ueda, pages 82 top, 87 bottom, 94 top left and right, 98 top, 104 top, and 112 top. The following images also are in the collection of the Gay Lesbian Bisexual Transgender Historical Society of Northern California: pages 46 bottom, 47 top, 52 bottom, 54 top, 59 bottom, 65 top, 66 bottom, 67 top, 71 bottom, 73 top, 76 top and bottom, 90 top, 93 top, 94 bottom right, 100 top, 106, and 117 bottom.

The photograph on page 127 of Troy Anicete, Mr. SF Leather 2004, and Bryan Ellis is by Anthony Abuzeide and for the Golden Gate Business Association's tourism campaign "Come Out Here." It is used with permission of the Golden Gate Business Association.

The photographs on pages 4, 109 top, and 111 top are by Greg Day, are © Greg Day, and are used with his kind permission. The image on page 101 bottom is by Mick Hicks for Rainbow25, © Mick Hicks/Rainbow 25. The photographs on pages 122 bottom, 123, 124, 125, and 126 are by Daniel Homsey and used with his kind permission. The photographs on pages 108 bottom, 119 top, 121 top, and 122 top are by Don Price and used with his kind permission. The image on page 119 bottom is used with permission of the San Francisco AIDS Foundation. The photograph on page 70 by Ray "Scotty" Morris and the photographs on pages 103 top and 104 bottom are copyright © the *San Francisco Examiner* and used with permission.

The following photographs and photographed items are in the collection of the San Francisco History Center, San Francisco Public Library: pages 43 top, 46 top, 48 top, 50 top, 53 top, 59 top, 60, 65 bottom, and 92 top.

Every effort has been made to determine and locate the copyright holders of images included in this book. Please contact the author at gayandlesbiansf@aol.com so proper credit may appear in any subsequent editions of this publication.

A book of this size unfortunately cannot possibly include or even acknowledge all of the organizations and individuals who have contributed to the development of the lesbian and gay community of San Francisco—some people simply by being themselves. There is much more to know about our past.

Except for the people who have publicly stated their sexual orientation, the inclusion in this publication of the name, image, likeness, or photograph of any individual should not be taken to indicate that he or she is homosexual, heterosexual, bisexual, transsexual, autosexual, or asexual.

FOREWORD

This has to be one of the most entertaining and informative pictorials on gay history yet. No matter what the decade or era, no matter the hairstyle or apparel (or lack thereof), there is something undeniably queer about all of them. Maybe it's the insouciance of the "French" postcards, with the artfully draped buff young men emulating mythical figures, which gives rise to the question, are they going to fight or make love? Or the cigar-chomping young women expressing both swagger and playfulness that does it. No matter, it does my gay heart good to see and feel what came before me and connect them to the photographs of the contemporary that I know so well.

One cannot help but feel strong pride in the contributions of so many gay men and lesbians—Julia Morgan, Dr. Marie Equip, Clarkson Crane—despite persecution and ridicule. San Francisco, so long identified with gays and lesbians, has been my home since 1962. Many of the changes I have witnessed are documented here in this book. My emotions range from exhilaration to sadness and, yes, even being turned on! Above all though is the undeniable aura of home, the hope that Harvey Milk always be talked about, the hope that various successes—political, social, personal—engender. A history filled with tragedy and frustration as well as victory and triumph. Milk was a contemporary of mine, and in many ways, his life and death here in San Francisco symbolizes much of what this book is about. A life and context that takes on operatic proportions. Milk possessed the *élan* that San Franciscans expect from their leaders. Like many, he came from another part of the country (in his case New York) wanting to experience the opportunity and hopeful liberation the city by the bay offered. He engaged the social and political scene hungrily, espousing social justice causes with passion. Gays, seniors, unionists, and others helped him make his mark as San Francisco's first openly gay elected official. Those were heady days and gave me the inspiration to be involved. His brutal murder and that of ally Mayor George Moscone in their city hall offices both traumatized the city and energized it. Dan White, the city supervisor, ex-cop, and fireman, who shot them in cold blood after receiving a slap on the wrist by the city's impotent criminal justice system, ended his on life ignominiously a few years later.

All this electricity and *strum und drag* are captured by the many riveting photographs in this book. It seems that no matter where gay men congregate, they practice the art of cruising. The furtive glance, the feigned indifference, all are part of an elaborate (if cursory) mating ritual. While in Paris, the Place due Concord is cited as such a location even in the 16th century, Wags have hissed that some of the men from then are still cruising today. Throughout the book, we can trace the mobility and variety of the best cruising places in San Francisco over the years: Union Square, the Presidio, upper market, and sundry parks and beaches.

Without the benefit of the Internet, cell phones, or faxes, the word was put out, and men would soon come flocking. When persecuted by law enforcement, they would set up shop elsewhere. Many of the busts by the police resulted in coverage that not only acknowledged the existence of gay activity but also titillated and resulted in more interest and creativity. I appreciate the book for giving these places their rightful station in queer history as it does the drag queens of both genders—flamboyant, haughty, beautiful, breaking boundaries, always pushing the envelope. They were and are essential to the evolvement of gay and lesbian civil rights. From Adam Isaacs Mencken to José Sarria, all impacted sensibilities and political advancement.

I was fascinated by all the foreshadowing and prescience illustrated in the book. Even in the mid- and late 1800s, you can find familiar subjects and causes. For instance, same-sex communities made of 40,000 transient and anonymous men; Heavens—I have the vapors! You could also find queer marriage, bull dykes, screaming drag, transvestites, transgender, fag hags, scandal, religion, S&M, and politics. Well you get the picture. Just think of those early pictures as the videotape of the time—San Francisco's queerest home videos.

While the right wing always thinks of the LGBT community as sexual only, our querulous selves always wanted room to grow, and San Francisco was the place. Artists, artisans, plumbers, cops, dancers, mule drivers, lawyers, city planners, bureaucrats, and eccentrics, all with a queer sensibility, nurtured and grew a culture. And what a culture it is, displayed in its full glory throughout *Gay and Lesbian San Francisco.*

Some of the most evocative photographs for me come from the 1960s through the present. My $40 transcontinental Greyhound bus trip in 1962 has paid me back a thousandfold, and I am not talking about money. The reproductions of the "homophile" organizations, with understandably self-conscious names such as The Society of Individual Rights or the Daughters of Bilitis, show its members looking ordinary, masking what we now acknowledge as sheer bravery and chutzpah. The evolvement in the 1970s to going public, civil disobedience, and trying to look anything but ordinary took on a hedonistic pace, all to a disco beat, are expertly captured. The painful 1980s, with the decimation caused by the HIV/AIDS epidemic, are painfully displayed through posters and fliers proclaiming a call to arms.

All in all, this is a book that you can pick up again and again, flipping through or reading closely, looking at it with friends, family, or by yourself. It sums up many changes and underlies the similarities of different eras. Mostly it is fun and informative, an important piece of lesbian and gay history here in San Francisco forever preserved. Let's see what the future holds.

—Tom Ammiano
Member, San Francisco Board of Supervisors

PREFACE

When it comes to the subject of gay and lesbian history, people too often adopt the stance of doubting Thomas. Sure Walt Whitman's poetry celebrates the "manly love of comrades," they say, but where is the smoking gun? Maybe Walt was just being effusive; let's not jump to wild conclusions! Of course, such evidentiary hurdles are not imposed when the subject of inquiry is affection between men and women. For example, Franklin Delano Roosevelt's affairs with women are hardly questioned, though not much mentioned, but the claim that Eleanor Roosevelt had equally passionate affairs with women is scoffed at. This historical denial of gay and lesbian lives and culture betrays a willful refusal to acknowledge the power and persistence of love.

Bill's book is an entertaining and thought-provoking response to this sour skepticism. He has amassed visual evidence that illustrates the long and storied history of gay and lesbian San Francisco. His playful, sometimes wry interpretation of this treasure trove of queer images is a solid addition to the history of one of America's greatest cities. From dancing gold miners to a lesbian marriage presided over by Sen. Dianne Feinstein, Bill brings to life a remarkable parade of characters, places, and events.

I've had the good fortune to be play a small role in helping Bill pursue this vital piece of cultural archeology. Many of the images that he features in this book come from the archives of the Gay, Lesbian Bisexual Transgender Historical Society, of which I am the executive director. For over 20 years, the GLBT Historical Society has built and maintained archives, sponsored programs and exhibits, and served as a center for research. A dedicated supporter and an engaged intellectual, Bill is a poster boy for the GLBT Historical Society's mission to increase public understanding, appreciation, and affirmation of the history and the culture of gay, lesbian, bisexual, transgender, and other sexual minority individuals and communities.

—Terence Kissack, Ph.D.
Executive Director, San Francisco Gay Lesbian Bisexual Transgender Historical Society

Here are two of the more than 150,000 men who passed through the Golden Gate on their way to the minefields during the gold rush. Levi Strauss and Company, founded in San Francisco in 1853 to supply miners with work clothes, began manufacturing its world-famous riveted jeans in 1873. Now known as 501s, they became essential to the "official Castro clone look" 100 years later once properly washed, faded, sanded, and stuffed.

One

A CITY OF MEN

Long before the city became the intergalactic headquarters of the Federation of Planets, *Life* magazine named San Francisco the "gay capitol of the world." Then a widely read and influential weekly publication, its June 26, 1964, issue sought to explain "homosexuality—and the problem it poses" to the general public for the first time. "Because of its reputation for easy hospitality," it stated, San Francisco "has a special appeal for them." The magazine did not mention it, but that "special appeal" seems always to have been there.

On January 1, 1848, the newly renamed village of San Francisco, with a population of perhaps 800 people, was a small, unimportant frontier settlement at the outer reaches of Mexico's California province. Within less than five years, everything changed for the tiny community. It not only became part of the United States, but the discovery of gold on the American River made it a major metropolis when more than 100,000 people from all over the world passed through it on their way to the mines. Because most were unmarried or traveling without their wives, San Francisco became a city of men.

More than 90 percent of the city's new inhabitants were men in their teens, 20s, 30s, and 40s. Some were Americans from the eastern United States—most of whom had never before been more than 25 miles from their homes and families—although the majority were not. They came from all parts of the world but especially from the west coast of Latin America, where news of the discovery was first to arrive. In time, they came from East Asia and eventually Europe as well.

Because they brought with them their ways of life, religious beliefs, habits, and mores, San Francisco immediately became a multicultural, cosmopolitan city. Between 1850 and 1860, more than half the population of San Francisco was foreign born; in other American cities, the number typically was no more than 10 percent.

The people of the gold rush understood sexuality differently than they do today. Concepts of homosexuality, bisexuality, and heterosexuality had not yet been invented, so people did not define themselves by their sexual orientation. Having intimate relations with a person of the same gender did not automatically make anyone into "a certain kind" of individual.

Americans especially believed in and encouraged intense, affectionate friendships between two people of the same gender, who often expressed their love for one another with great passion. Men who hugged and kissed other men in public and who wrote or spoke of their mutual deep feelings simply were demonstrating their ideal, pure, manly devotion to each other. Women who were "smashed on each other" were experiencing only a rite of passage that prepared them for marriage. At the time, someone referring to a "lover" might mean a person of his or her own gender; "sleep with" and "make love to" did not have specific sexual meanings.

All sexual intimacies outside of marriage were sinful, these "crimes against chastity," but during the gold rush "the preservation of virtue and dignity was a struggle as dispiriting as a San Francisco hill." Romantic friendship was so widely accepted that homoerotic acts were not noticed by the public or the police unless they were indiscrete. Between adults of the same gender, only sodomy was a crime. It was either so rare, so common, so unimportant, or so surreptitious that only a few Californians were ever in prison for it at the same time during the 19th century.

With few women in the city and even fewer in the mining camps, men undoubtedly turned to each other for comfort of all kinds. For some, in their physical and sexual primes, it may have been a matter of convenience only, but others certainly seized upon the opportunity to live exactly as they pleased, far from home and free of traditional social pressures.

Some gold-seeking Americans traveled to California by wagon train, but the vast majority arrived by clipper ships, which in 1849 departed eastern seaports for San Francisco at the rate of 130 or more a month.

For Americans, the sea voyage to San Francisco was extremely arduous. Even so, thousands of young men, leaving mostly from New York, paid $300 to $800 each to share cramped quarters on clippers for the 4- to 12-month sea voyage. The clippers lacked private cabins, so women were not allowed to sail with the miners-to-be in the first years.

Sex between seafarers was so common that it had its own name—boom cover trade—which referred to the physical intimacy sailors shared with each other under the tarps that protected ship's masts. Herman Melville, who knew first hand of such practices, called sailing vessels "wooden-walled Gomorrahs of the deep." By the end of 1849, when the city's earliest-known photograph (above) was taken, hundreds of vessels had been abandoned in Yerba Buena Cove with both passengers and sexually intimate crews off to the gold fields.

The oceangoing ships that brought the prospectors to California could not navigate the inland waterway to Sacramento, the natural jumping off point for the gold fields, so San Francisco became the great transfer center to the vessels. The city quickly became home to many anonymous and mostly transient men who stayed a few days or a few months before continuing their journeys.

In San Francisco, gold seekers found a city whose crowded boardinghouses, saloons, gambling clubs, public baths, busy waterfront, and congested streets made it easy for men with homoerotic desires to find each other. Those who did left no record of their intimacies, but in an age when women crocheted coverlets for piano legs, such propriety is not surprising; even the literate likely would not have written of such behavior.

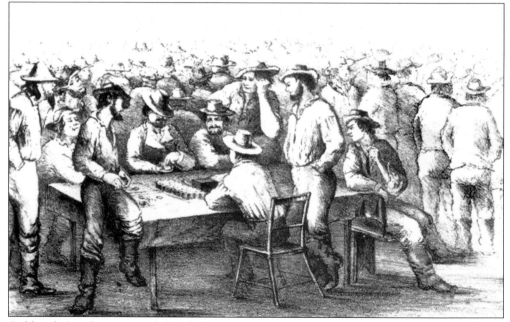

Gold rush San Francisco exhibited all the elements that encourage same-sex intimacy. There were few wives and fewer marriageable women. Female companionship was available, but it cost $200–$400 a night—$4,000 to $8,000 in today's dollars—which very few could afford. The probability of heterosexual relations for unmarried men was extremely small.

In gold rush days, "a woman walking along the streets of San Francisco was more of a sight than an elephant or giraffe would be today," noted one writer in 1873. When women finally moved to the city and merchants began importing finery for them, a few local cards took the opportunity to model recently arrived dress hoops.

Acting swiftly to regulate a new society, delegates like these met in September 1849 to draft a constitution for the State of California; voters approved it in December. Because it went into effect before California was admitted to the union, the document probably was not legally enforceable. It expressly forbade sodomy but did not specifically mention any other same-sex intimacy between consenting adults. The ban lasted until 1975.

Traveling to the mines from San Francisco, miners found even fewer women than they had seen in the city. In 1850, the federal census showed that there were 12 or more men to every woman in California, but in gold districts, the difference was even greater. Communities like Weaverville, Trinity County, had over 200 men and only one woman. Beals Bar had nearly 400 men and no women residents.

For many people, the gold rush turned 19th-century American gender roles inside out. Women who stayed behind now took on many of the responsibilities normally given to their husbands, sons, and fathers. Men who traveled to the mines also had to accept some traditional women's roles: cooking, housekeeping, and caring for the ill and injured.

California historian Hubert Howe Bancroft wrote, "New unions were made for mutual aid in danger, sickness, and labor. Scared like the marriage bonds, as illustrated by the softening of partner into the familiar 'pard,' were ties which oft united men vastly different in physique and temperament, the weak and the strong, the lively and sedate, thus yoking themselves together . . . with the heroic possibilities of a Damon or Patroclus," Achilles's lover.

The miners certainly knew that they would be residing in an essentially all-male society. Did any, already attracted to their own gender, leave home for the mines specifically to live as they desired sexually? That is not known, but other young men of the era voluntarily put themselves into all-male communities for months or years at a time where homoerotic relations occurred—work crews, military outposts, sailors, and others.

Living in extremely close proximity with each other, often sharing beds and blankets, who would be surprised if some of these men embraced each other for emotional or physical comfort? Many miners wrote in their diaries and letters home lamenting the lack of feminine influence, but others expressed pride in having created a world in which women, on a daily basis at least, had become essentially unnecessary.

Sundays were days of rest and recreation in the gold camps. The miners not only could take great pride in their appearance but great interest in the appearance of others and many of the men dressed up to look good for one another.

At occasional social events, some men agreed to "fill women's roles" by becoming the dancing partners of other men. It is not known if they remained so only for the length of a dance or for the entire evening, but apparently the men did not alternate between masculine and feminine parts during the evening.

The men "to be asked" identified themselves in different ways. At some camps, the better dressed became the "women." At others, men tied scarves around their arms to indicate they would take the woman's part. Elsewhere anyone "who had a patch on a certain part of his 'expressibles' "—typically a large square of canvas on a dark pair of pants—was willing to be invited to dance.

Did the "gentlemen" escort their "ladies" home? Did they leave them at the door or get invited in to spend the night? No one knows. Sex between men was not a crime, but it was a sin. Miners would not have written home about it any more than they would have about getting drunk, gambling, or other transgressions, including sexual relations with women not their wives. No one did.

With or without explicit records, homoerotic relations seem likely among some of the more than 150,000 men who came to California during the gold rush. Prevailing sentiment held that any sexual act outside marriage was sinful, but perhaps some kinds of sinfulness became irrelevant among at least some of the miners. It is irresponsible to suggest either that everyone abandoned their lifelong beliefs and behaviors or that no one reached for a friend under the covers at night. It is simply not known. What is certain is that the gold rush attracted a transient population of young men who were less likely to conform to social and sexual rules and regulations here than in their hometowns, some of whom may have come here specifically for the possibility to be themselves with each other.

The gold rush of the 1850s and the silver lode of the 1860s brought unimagined prosperity to San Franciscans and allowed many of them to enjoy life's fineries. For men, the height of fashion demanded a black silk frock coat with cloth buttons, a boiled shirt with a detachable wingtip collar, a satin bow tie, and a checkered waistcoat. No self-respecting gentleman put a crease in his pant legs. Required accessories included a gold pocket watch and chain and a hat appropriate for the time of day and occasion. Beards remained popular until the end of the century. For women, fashion required long, often trailing skirts, although the garments might be looped up for convenience when walking to the beach; cords and rings enabled them to be drawn up in festoons and led to a distinction between "walking" and "visiting" dresses. Crinoline remained the fabric of choice, but somewhat heavier materials were used in the 1860s; decoration was confined to the lower part of the skirt.

Two

BOHEMIA BY THE BAY

By the end of the gold rush, San Francisco had become the economic, social, and cultural capital of the western United States, "an oasis of civilization in the California desert." It supported numerous newspapers and literary journals, theaters, concert halls, and a thriving colony of people with artistic and literary interests who sought to disregard conventional standards of thought and behavior to become bohemians by the bay.

The men and women of the Gilded Age did not define themselves by their sexual acts and did not classify individuals as homosexual, bisexual, or heterosexual, as these terms did not exist until the end of the century. Even so, there were men who sought other men and women who sought other women.

People who would later be called gay or lesbian met each other through social networks, mutual friends, and wherever they could find and talk with each other, often with understood looks, coded language, gestures, and deniable conversation. At a time when sex of any type was a forbidden subject in polite society, homoromantic relationships, discretely hidden from view, did not create any controversy with the public or its protectors—they simply did not exist. Unmarried men, living alone or together, were "confirmed bachelors," and Sherlock Holmes and James Watson were the most famous. Spinsters lived together without arousing suspicion. What they could not do was write or talk about their sexual orientation publicly or live open lives.

Fortunately for the men and women able to recognize them, positive images of homoeroticism appeared occasionally. A short story, novel, or book of poetry might have a homoromantic theme. Unrecognized by the general public, a magazine might include a homoerotic illustration. Men especially, with the right connections, could read homoerotic, often pornographic literature by prominent authors. Mark Twain's poem, "The Mammoth Cod" was for private readership only, but he wrote "Some Thoughts on the Science of Onanism" for the Stomach Club:

> Of all the various kinds of sexual intercourse, this has the least to recommend it. As an amusement it is too fleeting; as an occupation it is too wearing; as a public exhibition there is no money in it.

His contemporary Eugene Field, best remembered for his verse for children, wrote the explicit "Socratic Love" so he could join the all-male Papyrus Club: "Now wit ye well that in those parts . . . 'twas not considered nasty . . . For sage philosophers to turn their tools to pederasty."

Born in 1843, Charles Warren Stoddard, San Francisco's first important gay author, arrived in the city with his family in 1855. He struggled professionally for a time—a requirement for a proper bohemian—until his story, "South Sea Idyll," published in the September 1869 issue of *Overland Monthly*, made him famous. It told of his relationship with a 16-year-old Tahitian boy, but most critics did not recognize its homoerotic content. During the next 50 years, it appeared in almost two dozen anthologies.

Stoddard chose not to live a public life as a someone we would call gay, but many well-known personalities, especially writers, artists, musicians, and actors, were authentic role models. Some of them lived in San Francisco. Others visited on national or international tours or on special occasions.

In his autobiographical novel, *For the Pleasure of His Company*, published in 1903, Stoddard offered insights into how he and other men found male lovers in San Francisco in the 1860s and 1870s. One way was through introductions by mutual friends, often women. In the story, Stoddard's hero met one lover through Little Mama. Another way was at parties; leaving for his lodgings after one gala, a new friend "invited Paul to accompany him and, without a moment's hesitation, the lad did so, and for a week following they were inseparable." In reality, Stoddard (below left) met artist Frank Millet (below right), a great romance of his life, in Venice. "We looked at each other," he later wrote, "and were acquainted in a minute." Mark Twain, whose secretary he was for a time, later wrote privately that Stoddard was "such a nice girl."

Stoddard also described how many men met through an interest in the theater. An actor, he wrote, "has his satellites, the type of young man who hangs about the theater, and is proud to be seen walking on the fashionable side of the afternoon pavement with the Mummer." His hero, when treading the boards, meets "a bright and well-bred lad who filled a clerkship dutifully during the day, but whose one pleasure in life was to spend his leisure hours in the society of his idol." When the photograph at right was taken of San Francisco's American Theater, the current production featured Laura Keene, whose performance Abraham Lincoln was watching the night he was assassinated. Ferdinand Gilbert's Melodeon offered more modest but reliable masculine entertainment, although no respectable woman would have entered it or its counterparts.

San Franciscans had a love of theatrical events from the beginning. The city's first concert took place on June 22, 1849, for an audience entirely of men. The first theater, Washington Hall, opened on January 16, 1850; the building later housed the city's "most elegant brothel." A more substantial structure, the Jenny Lind Theater on Portsmouth Square, above, became city hall in 1852.

Although Deuteronomy 22:5 expressly forbids cross-dressing as an "abomination unto the Lord," both female and male impersonators were extremely popular with pioneer San Franciscans, and Americans everywhere, who apparently raised no objection to any performer's violation of this particular scripture. Possibly the earliest to appear were the Bateman sisters, who during the 1850s toured in Shakespeare's *Richard III* with Ellen, 11, in the title role and Kate, 10, as Richmond.

Mrs. John Wood first performed in San Francisco is 1858, primarily in burlesques and operettas. Among other roles, she played a graceful gallant in *The Corsair* and the hero in *Don Leander* (right). After successful careers as both an actress and a theater manager, she retired from the stage in 1905.

By the end of the 1850s, minstrels were among the city's most popular stage attractions. Adding insult to injury with their heavily biased and ultimately contemptuous view of African Americans, some troops wore both blackface and drag to perform transvestite burlesques of popular plays and operettas, including *Macbreath* and *Patients; or Bunion-salve's Bride*. Many people considered the San Francisco Minstrels, seen here, the best of all.

27

Adam Isaacs Mencken, the most sensational actress of her day, reached San Francisco in 1863 for a long engagement of sold-out performances in *Back-Eyed Susan* (above left), *The French Spy* (above right), and *Mazeppa* (below left), all "pants parts." To Charles Stoddard, "She was a vision of celestial harmony made manifest in the flesh." She delighted in visiting the city's casinos and brothels in men's clothing.

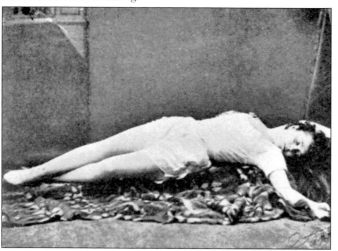

After leaving San Francisco, Mencken (at right, standing) eventually journeyed to Europe where she met author George Sand (seated). Both favored short hair, cigars, and—when they dined together—wearing men's clothes. Sand, wrote Mencken, "So infuses me with the spirit of life that I cannot bear to spend an evening apart from her." The actress married four times, but many contemporaries believed the women's relationship was intimate in every way.

For women with the wealth to afford it and the wherewithal to ignore what others thought about them socially or sexually, male attire became popular during the Gilded Age. San Francisco's own Lotta Crabtree (left and right) not only enjoyed wearing men's clothes and smoking their cigars, which she did all her life, she liked to be photographed doing both. At the peak of her career, she was America's highest-paid actress. Among her contemporaries, beloved, eccentric Lillie Hitchcock Coit (below) also smoked cigars and favored a night on the town in masculine attire. Romantically linked to many men, Crabtree never wed, but Coit's marriage lasted 22 years, until her husband's death.

Before turning to the dramatic stage in the 1860s, Polish contralto Felicita Vestvali specialized in operatic roles previously reserved for men—Tancred, Orfeo, and Figaro. She played Shakespeare's Romeo, a signature part, for the first time in San Francisco, which was already known for its appreciation of transvestite performance. Her contemporary, Rosa von Braunschweig, believed Vestvali's later success was due to her friendship with a German actress that lasted until her death in 1880.

When male impersonator Ella Wesner first performed in San Francisco in 1871, she "bewitched the town." The *Figaro*, a local paper, regretted that "ladies can't go to the Bella Union, they would all fall in love with (her)." She was especially beloved by all-male, working-class audiences. Wesner never married, although gossip linked her romantically to robber baron Jim Fisk's mistress after his death.

Wesner's great success inspired other performers to emulate her. Some had long careers, but at least one ended tragically. In 1876, five years after Wesner's visit, a male impersonator appearing in San Francisco was shot and killed by a man who found her in bed with his fiancée. "A woman's mania for wearing male attire ends in death," headlined the *New York Clipper*, discretely masking the truth.

During the same period, female impersonator Paul Vernon became one of San Francisco's most popular vaudevillians. He and others were accepted by their largely male audiences because they saw any personal femininity as simply "a very finished piece of acting;" any masculinity of male impersonators also was just part of the characterization. Only portrayals of "a certain class of effeminate young man" in male clothes were considered distasteful.

In his autobiography, San Francisco native Lincoln Steffens described "an ancient, highly organized system of prostitution" at the local military academy he attended in the 1870s. It also existed elsewhere. One student had "a large number of the little boys" and "let them out to other older boys at so much money, candy, or credit per night." Eventually the school ended "the fagging system and, too, the vice foundation thereof."

Oscar Wilde visited San Francisco in 1882, giving a series of lectures about "The English Renaissance," "Art Decoration," and "The House Beautiful." He received a blizzard of Wednesday editorial and Sunday sermon denunciations for his "sunflower aestheticism," which included his knee britches, velvet coat, lace cuffs, and catch phrases such as "too utterly utter," "just too too," and "do you yearn?"

When the *Wasp* characterized Wilde in an editorial cartoon as a false, fawning "sunflower messiah," it included many prominent San Franciscans in the crowd. The *San Francisco News Letter* described a more typical aficionado: he "is the pink of perfection; he receives $80 per month as an under-clerk in the wholesale grocery;"—such positions then considered suitable only for effeminate men—"he wears a claw-hammer coat, with satin lapels, at all evening entertainments, and stands off his celestial wringer of linens with an indignant and aristocratic air; he reads Rosetti and Wilde and Swinburne, and other authors of the aesthetic school; he is seldom seen without a *boutonniere*, and aims to wear fresh ones daily, and proudly swells with the impression that he is just too too utterly utter in his utterances."

San Franciscans continued to follow Wilde's career. After his conviction for "abnormal sexual vice" in 1895, a group of University of California students interrupted a performance of Gilbert and Sullivan's *Patience* when an actor impersonating Wilde (behind the telescope) appeared on stage. The Palace Hotel, where Wilde had stayed and been feted during his visit, deleted his name—but not the menu—from his page in its banquet book.

Sarah Bernhardt, possibly the finest emotional actress of the Gilded Age, came to San Francisco on five separate tours between 1887 and 1918. On stage, she moved easily between women and men's roles, most famously as the title characters in *Camille* and *Hamlet* (left). Offstage she moved just as easily between affairs with women and men, making no secret of any.

Loie Fuller caused a sensation when she first performed her innovative modern dances in San Francisco in 1896. Three years later, she met Gab Sorere (nee Bloch), who became her lover and collaborator for the rest of her long career; they founded an all-woman dance company in 1907. In 1915, they returned to the city to perform at the Panama-Pacific International Exposition.

CALIFORNIA THEATRE

AL. HAYMAN CO. (INCORPORATED), Proprietors

LA LOIE FULLER

When Julian Eltinge appeared at San Francisco's Cort Theater in 1912 in *The Fascinating Widow*, he was the most famous and extraordinary cross-dresser in the world. He published the *Julian Eltinge Magazine of Beauty Hints and Tips*, endorsed a line of corsets, and marketed his own cold cream, liquid whiting, and powder. Lured to Hollywood, he was more successful than any other female impersonator in film, except Lassie.

According to *Variety*, San Francisco's own Bothwell Browne was second only to Julian Eltinge as a female impersonator. His famed vaudeville act of exotic dances, which debuted at the city's Hippodrome in 1916, featured him as Cleopatra in *The Vampire of the Nile*. When it opened in New York, *Variety* called it "the best staged, produced, costumed and elaborate dancing turn that ever left the Pacific Coast."

During the Gilded Age, men seeking men in San Francisco could find each other in places besides theaters. By the 1890s, such establishments included many of the city's Turkish baths, although none operated exclusively for gays until the 1930s. Some may have been home base for male prostitutes, and many "traditional" houses of prostitution also might have included at least one young man for customers interested in male-male sex.

Anywhere in the city, men could identify themselves to each other through appearance, gestures, and ambiguous conversations of coded messages—all vital means of communication that became part of an emerging culture. In Oscar Wilde's day, green carnations were popular symbols for the like-minded. By the turn of the 20th century, red neckties—the customer in the postcard on the right is wearing one—had replaced them. Looks and attitudes also were part of the discrete, secret discussion, although judging from some of the postcards of the period (the one below was part of a larger series), they were not all that secret.

Almost no documentation exists about the underside of gay life in San Francisco before the turn of the 20th century, although a brief entry in the record books of one local businessman provides some insight, "W. C., sherry dealer in town from London. Wanted a boy today . . . Got doorman at _____ to arrange meeting at _____'s Turkish Bath." Presumably such arrangements could be made through people holding similar positions at other hotels.

During the Spanish-American War of 1898, San Francisco became both a major embarkation point for troops going to the Philippines and a major embarrassment for the military command when soldiers began supplementing their pay through male prostitution. "Amiable young soldiers were to be 'had' so plentifully that their fees consequently fell." Authorities moved to end the activity as quickly as possible.

By the turn of the 20th century, the city had a number of places where men met each other for sex: Union Square, Ocean Beach, and Land's End, but especially the waterfront of the Embarcadero and lower Market Street, where saloons catered to a transient clientele of seafarers and others.

Men who knew where to find them could buy erotic paintings, drawings, and photographs, some completely explicit. The least expensive were "French" postcards, misnamed because they could not be mailed, German stereo cards (left)—this one amended by the publisher with some tasteful drapery—"art studies," and pictures of ancient statuary. Photographic images of women loving each other (right) also were produced, but probably were not for sale to them.

Sometimes the girls kiss each other in

San Francisco

but it's only between times

As long as the women on a postcard, "French" or otherwise, were fully dressed, apparently the United States Post Office would accept it, as it did this one in 1910.

Women who loved women were even more invisible than men in the 19th and early 20th century. Schoolgirl crushes and "romantic friendship" were accepted, but women were expected to marry. Few would have questioned two "spinsters" living together, but with limited professional choices, many had no option but to wed. These two women may have been in a committed relationship or simply clowning for the camera.

A gift to the street, local artist Douglas Tilden's *Mechanic's Monument* was installed on Market Street in 1904. With its five near-nude machinists—not recommended for actual foundry work—it is an outstanding example of his art, which typically portrays muscular young men. Once a year, it additionally is adorned with live young men who climb up for a view of the city's Pride Parade.

In 1904, Julia Morgan, the first woman to be registered as an architect in California, opened her first office in San Francisco. In 1919, she was hired to build Hearst Castle in San Simeon, her most famous project. By the time she retired in 1951, she had designed more than 700 buildings.

41

In Willa Cather's "Paul's Case," published in 1905, Paul, a doomed adolescent aesthete, wears a red carnation during his visit to New York City. He meets "a wild boy from San Francisco," with whom he spends a night on the town. Cather gives no reason, but they part coldly; perhaps one of them misunderstood a subtle meaning. The story has been anthologized in high school English texts ever since.

Among the humanitarians who hastened to San Francisco after the great earthquake and fire of 1906, Dr. Marie Equi received a commendation from the U.S. Army for her work. Ironically the government later convicted her of sedition because she urged men not to enlist during World War I. At her trial, her prosecutors submitted evidence of her lesbianism in an attempt to portray her as morally corrupt.

The Dash, the city's first known homoerotic dance hall, opened on the Barbary Coast at 574 Pacific Avenue in 1908. Owned by a clerk of the municipal court and featuring "degenerate female impersonators," it was quickly closed in the reform movement that followed the disasters of 1906. Spider Kelly's Tivoli Café, next door to the Schivo Brothers' Hippodrome, occupies the site in this photograph taken a few years later.

Famed composer Camille Saint-Saens journeyed to San Francisco in 1915 to conduct his "Ode to California," commissioned by the city's Panama-Pacific International Exposition as its official composition. Usually he favored more exotic destinations like Egypt and Morocco, where he went as much for the rendezvous as for the resorts. He denied he was a homosexual. "No, my dear," he claimed, "I am a pederast."

The year of the exposition, Alexander Berkman spoke in San Francisco about homosexuality, possibly the city's first lecture on the subject and among its earliest public defenses in the United States. A lifelong anarchist and convicted felon for the attempted murder of Henry Clay Frick, he was found guilty of conspiracy to obstruct the operation of the selective service law during World War I and was deported in 1919.

The national press provided positive gay images occasionally, although some men may have found their interest in them disquieting rather than comforting. These Ivory Soap ads appeared in 1916 and 1919 issues of *National Geographic*. To anyone so inclined, their homoeroticism was unmistakable, even when no one knew that the artist, J. C. Leyendecker, was gay. He and his partner were together for 50 years.

During the Great War, with vast numbers of temporary barracks built near the Palace of Fine Arts, the Presidio again became a popular cruising site, a practice the military moved immediately to suppress; for the first time, it discharged men for homosexual behavior. The military also instigated a raid on the Baker Street Club, a pair of flats where new friends could find a few hours of privacy. It closed immediately.

Born in Pennsylvania, raised in Oakland and San Francisco, and later living in Paris, Gertrude Stein (left) began early in the 20th century to write about lesbianism as normal and natural. Her *Tender Buttons*, published in 1914, was unabashed lesbian eroticism, beginning with its punning title. Even for those who did not read her work, she and her lifelong partner, Alice Toklas (right), born in San Francisco, became important role models.

Built for the men of the waterfront, and any men who wished to use its facilities, the Embarcadero YMCA opened in 1924 to provide clean hotel rooms at reasonable prices for more than 50 years. Many of the city's first gay bars, baths, and clubs started nearby in the next decade.

When Clarkson Crane's novel of San Francisco and Berkeley, *The Western Shore*, appeared in 1925, it was notable for several reasons: it was published by a mainstream American press; it presented its gay characters as people, not stereotypes; several speculated openly about one character's "tendencies in love;" and none met a tragic fate. Crane (left) and his lover Clyde Evans (right) were lifelong friends of poet Elsa Gidlow.

Elsa Gidlow moved to San Francisco in 1926, three years after her *On a Grey Thread* appeared, the first book of openly lesbian poetry published in the United States. Her wide circle of creative friends included Robinson Jeffers, Kenneth Rexroth, and Clarkson Crane.

During most of the 1920s, the police paid only minimal attention to the city's gay men, many of whom met each other along the Embarcadero and lower Market Street. The department's unstated policy was essentially to ignore them unless someone complained. That policy would change dramatically in the next decade.

Because of increasing awareness during the 1930s, the police department added plainclothes officers to its parks and squares unit to keep the "fruiters" in check. They began surveillance of the known places where gay men might go to meet each other, such as Union Square, the basement of the City of Paris, Hamilton Square in the Western Addition, and Golden Gate Park (left). They also started sting operations in the Silver Palace Theater on Market Street (below), where a customer might make a pass at a decoy working for one of the officers who would then arrest him. At the same time, the brutality of young men who drove around the city looking for gays to beat up was regarded by many locals as "a manly expression of high spirits."

Three

AN EMERGING VISIBILITY

By the beginning of the 1930s, homosexuality was widely viewed as an abnormality. The term itself had first been used toward the end of the 19th century, but it did not truly reach the American public until after the *New York Times* printed it for the first time in 1926. By then, the relatively new field of psychiatry, which viewed same-sex relationships as abnormal, had become a popular fashion.

The growing dislike of homosexuality was part of a shift away from the perceived "moral laxity" of the Roaring Twenties that permitted, among other non-traditional behaviors, sexual liberation and experimentation. It also was part of the response to the social and economic changes created by the Great Depression of the 1930s, when many men not only lost their jobs but also their place as economic head of the family, a key challenge to their manhood.

The gay men and lesbians who were noticed by the general public seemed to fit the most blatant stereotypes of previous generations—effeminate men and masculine women. They appeared in popular fiction and especially motion pictures. Written and set in San Francisco, Dashell Hammett's *The Maltese Falcon* was unusual because it contained three gay characters, not just one. The novel, stereotypes included, became so successful it was filmed 3 times in 10 years (1931, 1936, and 1941).

Film, then the most popular visual medium, reflected the social views of homosexuals. The ideal male changed from the "softer," sensitive, somewhat gender-ambiguous heros personified by such stars as Rudolph Valentino, Ramon Novarro, Norman Kerry, Rod LaRocque, and John Gilbert to the powerful, forceful, and sexually confident leading men played by Clark Gable, James Cagney, and others. After the Production Code went into effect on July 1, 1934, depictions of homosexuals and references to homosexuality itself became specifically banned from all American motion pictures.

Only stereotypes of lesbians and gays survived the new prohibition. In movies of the 1930s, hotel managers, valets, waiters, dressmakers, and department store clerks always seemed to have arched eyebrows, mincing walks, sharp tongues, and an aversion to women. Did any film of the period have a repressed schoolmarm, an old maid, a female prison warden or predatory matron of women who was not tall, large, and deep-voiced? The studios might claim that the roles were not created with any sexuality in mind, but to the audience these characters represented homosexuals.

Despite such attempts to make not only homosexuals, but homosexuality, disappear, San Francisco's lesbians and gays blossomed after the repeal of Prohibition. Even though laws forbade them from gathering openly with heterosexuals in licensed restaurants and bars, being served liquor, or dancing or touching each other, gays and lesbians owned and frequented a number of successful bars and clubs in different parts of the city during the 1930s. The best known were in North Beach, but by the end of the decade they also were along the Embarcadero, on Market Street, and near Union Square.

Stereotyping and discrimination became particularly difficult for gays and lesbians during the 1940s, when the military, for the first time, began screening its personnel to keep out and weed out anyone who might be homosexual. To "avoid corruption of enlisted men and women," they declared some bars and restaurants off-limits and worked with the police to enforce the ban. Instead of improving after the war ended, however, the inequity only got worse.

San Francisco's best-known lesbian and gay bars were in North Beach. Looking west on Broadway in this image, Mona's, then the city's most popular women's club, is on the right. Finocchio's, world famous for its drag performances, was less than a block away. The Black Cat was a few blocks south of both.

Opened originally in 1906 at Mason and Eddy Streets (left), the Black Cat Café was known for its bohemian nonconformity and outlandish entertainment even before it moved to 710 Montgomery in North Beach (right) in 1933. There it became the most famous bohemian gathering place in San Francisco, attracting writers, artists, and musicians—both straight and gay—many of whom lived in the neighborhood.

In 1933, the year the Black Cat relocated, police raided Tati's Café to close down "Frisco city's first pansy show," *Boys Will Be Girls*, with female impersonator Rae Bourbon (right). Because the show was being broadcast, the raid became the first carried live on local radio. "Rough Frisco Cops Send Pinched Boys to Women's Court," reported *Variety*.

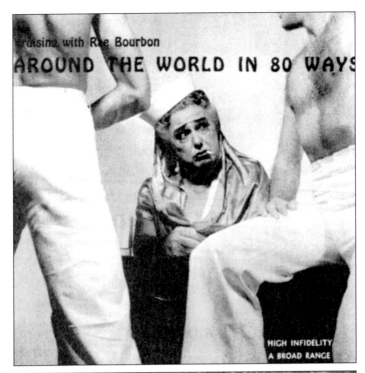

Cruising with Rae Bourbon

AROUND THE WORLD IN 80 WAYS

HIGH INFIDELITY
A BROAD RANGE

Opened as a small Bohemian café and speakeasy in 1929 at 406 Stockton, Finocchio's moved to 506 Broadway in 1936. Given its owners' real last name, Italian slang for "pouf" or "pansy," it became the most famous and flamboyant of all the city's night spots where gays and lesbians, open and obvious, mixed with a crowd of celebrities and tourists.

Plainclothes police raided Finocchio's in 1936, just before its move to North Beach. They arrested 10 people, including the owners, but only two female impersonators were convicted, for singing "vulgar and ribald songs," and sentenced to 30 days in jail. One was future Finocchio's star Walter Hart. He became famous for his impression of Sophie Tucker, who adored him and occasionally sent him one of her gowns.

Mona's, San Francisco's first lesbian bar, opened on Union Street in 1934 before moving to 140 Columbus in North Beach in 1936. Three years later, it moved again, this time to 440 Broadway, where it featured male impersonators. In 1948, it moved, for the last time, to nearby 473 Broadway. It closed in 1957.

Owned and managed by Mona Sargent, the bar became extremely popular with women, which brought the police for an inspection. Arrested in 1937 for keeping a "disorderly house," a common charge against gay and lesbian club owners, Mona wound up in jail overnight but still looked fabulous.

During World War II, unprecedented numbers of servicemen and women passed through San Francisco, many learning about themselves and each other for the first time. Built in 1941, the city's Hospitality House hosted more than a million men in its first 12 months alone. Its one-year anniversary celebration attracted "10,000 men in uniform and invited girls" to the Civic Auditorium, where they heard greetings from California governor Culbert Olson.

Enlisted men could meet local residents, and each other, at bars in the Tenderloin along the Embarcadero and Market Street and around Union Square. In 1942, the California State Board of Equalization warned the Old Crow and more than 50 other bars in San Francisco that they risked losing their liquor licenses if they did not "conform strictly to the State liquor laws;" two were closed almost immediately.

Many military personnel, especially officers, preferred more upscale establishments like the Top of the Mark, where they could meet other men without fear of becoming caught in a raid of a "queer" bar. The cocktail lounge was cited by the Board of Equalization in 1942, but it was not subject to surprise invasions by the police.

The city's civilian population also increased dramatically during the war, with new jobs in factories and shipyards attracting tens of thousands of people. Production became intense. By 1944, the Bay Area led the world in shipbuilding. Women especially had opportunities previously denied them, eventually becoming one-third of all Liberty Ship workers. Experiencing social and financial independence for the first time, many stayed after the war ended.

The number of lesbian and gay establishments grew with the influx of military personnel and civilians, but the war also increased the persecution of gays and lesbians. The military declared almost 100 bars and clubs in San Francisco to be off-limits, including the Black Cat, where military police, seen here at the back of the bar, made sure soldiers did not violate the ban.

BUNA BATHTUB

"We came across this Buna village," says a private in the army.

Millions of Cannon Towels

are now going to the Armed Forces. So you may find a smaller selection in the stores — fewer styles and a limited variety of colors. But the durable Cannon quality, the hardy quality that will see you through, remains the same. Cannon will...

During World War II, for the first time, the military actively sought to keep gay men from serving in the armed forces, asking recruits, "Are you homosexual?" and dishonorably discharging those it found among its troops. At the same time, it encouraged male bonding and allowed social interactions between soldiers that often seemed identical to many of society's stereotypes of gay behaviors. Such conduct might have been questioned in civilian life, but it was so common and accepted during the war that a towel company presented it in a series of ads in *Life* magazine to sell its product.

ARMY DAY — CROCODILES KEEP OUT!

Illustration as described by the Army Medico

Did you ever have to put a net across your bathtub — and share it with a crocodile? Sometimes, according to this medical corps captain, you have to do that for a bath — in the South Pacific Islands.

Millions of Cannon Towels

are now going to the Armed Forces. So you may find a smaller selection in the stores — fewer styles and a limited variety of colors. But the durable Cannon quality...

Women were not asked about their sexual orientation by the military until 1944, when it put procedures in place to screen out lesbians. By then, the popular imagination had changed to let women take jobs that previously had been "for men only" and a new, more masculine image, "Rosie the Riveter," became iconic. Many women met their first partners working in war factories.

During the 1940s, Gladys Bentley performed at Mona's 440 Club, off-limits to military personnel, wearing an all-white tuxedo and top hat. Openly lesbian, she appeared earlier in her career backed by a chorus of men in drag. Poet Langston Hughes called her the "Brown Bomber of Sophisticated Songs" and "an amazing exhibition of musical energy." She also was renowned for inventing ribald lyrics to popular tunes.

When San Francisco poet Robert Duncan's 1944 essay, "The Homosexual in Society," appeared in the journal *Politics*, he became the first American man to come out publicly. He made the then extraordinary claim that homosexuals were a persecuted minority, although he championed "devotion to human freedom" and "the liberation of human love" rather than a specific gay rights movement. Duncan died in San Francisco in 1988.

By the end of the war, lesbian and gay life in San Francisco had changed dramatically. Circles of friends and private gatherings were no longer the only ways for women or men to socialize. They now had clubs, bars, restaurants, and, for men at least, bathhouses. They also now had beliefs about themselves and their country based upon the goals of the war.

After World War II, Union Square became the hub of a sprawl of social establishments that catered to gay and lesbian customers, stretching to North Beach, South of Market, the Tenderloin, and Polk Street. Union Square also became a casual meeting place for men, as did Market Street from the cable-car turnaround at Powell Street to the Civic Center.

Those who may have looked forward to greater freedom would be disappointed. "San Francisco is rapidly becoming the central gathering-point of lesbians and homo-sexuals in California," warned *The Truth* in its July 11, 1949, issue, due to "the green light that we have given [them] to practice their quirks in our fair city." The persecution of the previous two decades would only intensify during the 1950s.

World War II had a greater impact on San Francisco's lesbian and gay community than any event since the gold rush. Hundreds of thousands of men and women visited the city during the conflict or came for work in the Bay Area's war industries, and many decided to live here permanently after the war. Some of the new lesbian and gay residents moved into what was then known as San Francisco's Central City Ghetto, an area straddling Market Street that included the Tenderloin and what was then known as South of the Slot. It created a neighborhood that included not only bars and restaurants but political and social organizations and even a community center, the nation's first.

Four

HOMOPHILES AND HOMOPHOBES

After World War II, the political and social climate of opinion in the United States became increasingly conservative and conformist. The same had happened after World War I, when the government targeted communists and foreigners. Now it singled out communists and homosexuals.

Accused or suspected communists were blacklisted, but no one kept a similar list of known homosexuals because homosexuality itself was blacklisted. In 1952, the American Psychiatric Association declared it to be a sociopathic personality disturbance. At the same time, researchers at San Francisco's Langley Porter Clinic, offering hope of a cure, published "The Problem of Homosexuality," which examined the usefulness of castration, lobotomy, and electroshock treatment for homosexuals. Many similar studies appeared during the next two decades.

In 1953, Pres. Dwight Eisenhower issued Executive Order 10450, banning "sexual perverts" from government employment, and within two years more than 800 federal employees were fired because of their sexual orientation. Adopted by state and local governments, the exclusion eventually covered 20 percent of the workforce. Known or presumed homosexuals joined a remarkable group of Americans blacklisted for a variety of reasons. Some members were gay (Leonard Bernstein, Aaron Copland, Will Geer, and Langston Hughes), and some were not (Lena Horne, Gypsy Rose Lee, Paul Robeson, Orson Welles).

In an era when the father on a television show always wore a tie, even around the house; when the mother always wore a dress to cook and wash dishes; when an episode of a prime-time, long-running series could have a plot of nothing more than, "Wally and Lumpy are looking for Beaver," the nation's moral guardians expected conformity in beliefs and behaviors and viewed lesbians and gays as especially dangerous to social stability. Their goal became a "purge of the perverts."

To combat the "homosexual threat," California changed its penal code in 1949 so the state "approves and recognizes only one method of sexual intercourse. That method is the relationship between the sex organ of a man and the sex organ of a woman. . . . Other practices are here classified as 'unnatural' in the sense that they are proscribed by law."

The same year, the State Board of Equalization suspended the Black Cat's liquor license because it claimed that the club was serving "persons with known homosexual tendencies." Upon appeal, the California State Supreme Court in 1951 ordered the license restored for two reasons. First it stated that homosexuals had the right to gather in public places for social reasons. Second it said no evidence of "illegal or immoral conduct on the premises" had been presented.

State and local agencies eventually discovered they could "create" illegal conduct by defining it to include same-sex dancing, kissing, hand-holding, and hugging by patrons as proof of an establishment's immoral character. They also learned they could use decoys and undercover agents to arrest patrons for illegal acts, even when the acts had not actually taken place. By 1955, the crackdown on gays in San Francisco was in full swing.

In response to similar actions, homosexuals in most parts of the country went deeply into their closets, but not in San Francisco, where some opposed the repression and fought for their rights. Perhaps these men and women who had lived through the war years wished for themselves the freedoms for which the war had been fought. Perhaps their youthful idealism led them to believe they could make a difference. For whatever reason, San Francisco saw the emergence of a lesbian and gay rights movement in the midst of tremendous persecution of anyone different.

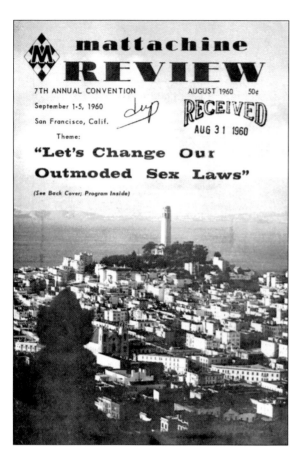

The Mattachine Society was founded in Los Angeles in 1950 and began publishing the *Mattachine Review*, its nationally distributed journal, in San Francisco in 1954. It moved its headquarters to the city three years later. Named after Mattacino, a kind of court jester in Italian theater who spoke the truth to the king when nobody else would, its primary goal was public understanding and acceptance of homosexuality.

Started in San Francisco in 1955 by Del Martin, Phyllis Lyon, and six other women, the Daughters of Bilitis, the first lesbian civil rights and social organization in the United States, fought for legal reform and gay civil rights, hosted public forums on homosexuality, and participated in research activities. *The Ladder*, its monthly magazine, began publication in 1956.

THE LADDER

Monthly magazine of articles, stories, poems, book reviews, quotes, comment and significant opinion on sexual problems facing the Lesbian in society today. Published by The DAUGHTERS OF BILITIS, Inc., non-profit educational, research and social service organization. Subscriptions mailed in sealed plain envelope, $2.50.

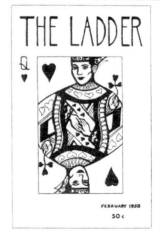

DAUGHTERS OF BILITIS

165 O'Farrell Street, Suite 405   San Francisco 2, Calif.

Telephone YUkon 2-9290

In 1955, San Francisco police, enforcing the conformity of the times, arrested J. C. "Bunny" Breckenridge for wearing a "woman's hairdo" and "flamboyant clothing" in public. A wealthy direct descendant of John Cabell Breckenridge, the 14th vice president of the United States, he survived the scandal to portray the Ruler (right) in Edward D. Wood Jr.'s science-fiction classic, *Plan 9 From Outer Space*, his only film appearance.

Throughout the 1950s, the Alcohol Beverage Control Board and the San Francisco police continued to raid lesbian and gay bars, citing disorderly conduct. In 1956 alone, they once again invaded the Black Cat; suspended the liquor licenses of Ethel's, the Crossroads, the Copper Lantern, and the Paper Doll; and revoked the license of Miss Smith's Tea Room. Police also used vagrancy laws to harass gays.

During the 1950s, bohemian North Beach was the center of the Beat movement, which included, from left to right, Bob Danlon, Neal Cassady, Allen Ginsberg, Robert LaVigne, and Laurence Ferlinghetti. Ginsberg wrote his most famous poem, *Howl*, in San Francisco, which Ferlinghetti published. In 1957, they were tried for selling obscene literature because of the work's descriptions of male homosexuality. Ginsberg became America's most important eligible poet not to win a Pulitzer Prize.

Allen Ginsberg called the Black Cat "the greatest gay bar in America." During the 1950s, José Sarria was the club's most popular performer, and his Sunday afternoon drag operas were its most popular attraction. He closed every show leading the audience in a rendition of "God Save Us Nelly Queens," to the music of "America," an important political statement during a repressive decade.

The Black Cat Opera Association celebrated its first anniversary in 1959 with a production of *Madame Butterfly*, the first opera it had done. Sarria played the title role, and Sol Stoumen, the bar's heterosexual owner, appeared as Pinkerton, Butterfly's lover. Alexander Anderson, the show's costume and scenery designer, did this sketch for the extravaganza's poster. After fighting police harassment for years, the bar closed in 1963.

San Francisco's gays and lesbians became the central issue of 1959's municipal election when city assessor Russell Wolden, running for mayor, accused incumbent George Christopher (center, with his campaign managers Joseph Alioto, left, and Walter Haas) of letting the city become "the national headquarters of organized homosexuals in the United States." So many people resented his raising "the shoddy issue of homosexuality" that he lost by a wide margin.

65

After Mayor Christopher's reelection, police raids of homosexual bars intensified, reaching an apex, although not an end, in 1961 with the arrest of 89 men and 14 women at the Tay-Bush. One judge, branding San Francisco a "Parisian pansy's paradise," threatened harsh penalties for any homosexuals brought before him. The court dismissed the case against owner Robert Johnson (left, at his arraignment) when he agreed to close his business.

JOSÉ JULIO SARRIA, Candidate for Supervisor
City and County of San Francisco
November 7, 1961

My Platform is Completely and Eloquently Engraved for All Time on the Facade of San Francisco's New **HALL OF JUSTICE** TO THE FAITHFUL AND IMPARTIAL ENFORCEMENT OF THE LAWS ⋆ WITH EQUAL AND EXACT JUSTICE TO ALL ⋆ OF WHATEVER STATE OR PERSUASION ⋆ THIS BUILDING IS DEDICATED BY THE PEOPLE OF THE CITY AND COUNTY OF SAN FRANCISCO

In 1961, public policies of discrimination and harassment prompted José Sarria to become the first openly gay man to run for office in the United States. He had difficulty finding 25 people willing to sign his nominating petition, but almost 7,000 voted for him for supervisor in the privacy of the polling booth and showed the possibility of a gay voting bloc for the first time.

The same year, José Sarria and Guy Strait founded the League for Civil Education (LCE) to develop a political voice for gays in the city. Its *LCE News*, published weekly, was the city's first gay newspaper. The organization disbanded in 1964.

LCE

LEAGUE FOR CIVIL EDUCATION
1154 KEARNY   SAN FRANCISCO   SU. 1-2940

MEMBERSHIP CERTIFICATE

THIS IS TO CERTIFY THAT

William M. Plath

IS A MEMBER IN GOOD STANDING. TO AND INCLUDING JUNE 30, 1962.

INCORPORATED

PRESIDENT

SECRETARY   SEAL

8 June 19 61   No. 4604   APRIL 24, 1961

The League for Civil Education was formed for educational, benevolent, charitable, and philanthropic purposes; and the specific and primary purposes for which it was formed are to defend,   and protect civil rights and liberties guarant   stitution of the United States and of the State   to sponsor and promote a continuing educ   the field of civil rights and liberties; to prov   aid for the defense or protection of persons whose   onal rights have been violated or are threatened or imperiled, to provide and promote opportunities and referral services free from discrimination of any kind in connection with employment placement, housing placement, and personal counselling, and to support and contribute to worthy charitable and civic endeavors.

BOOT PARTY THURSDAYS

W H Y N O T

**518 ELLIS
PR. 6-3333**

Before the Why Not?, the city's first leather bar, opened in the Tenderloin in 1961, leathermen had mostly patronized waterfront bars such as Jacks, the Sea Cow, and the Castaways. Although it lasted only a year, the Why Not? showed there was a leather community in San Francisco that could support its own establishments.

The Tool Box, the first leather bar located South of Market, opened at Fourth Street and Harrison in 1962. It became world famous when *Life* magazine featured it and the Jumpin' Frog on Polk Street in an article, "Homosexuality in America," published in its June 26, 1964, issue. The same year, the Big Glass opened on Fillmore, the first black-owned and black-oriented gay bar in San Francisco.

In addition to any other celebrity, the Tool Box was well known for it huge mural, painted in black and white by Chuck Arnett. *Life* used two pages to present it in its article, describing "A San Francisco bar run for and by homosexuals . . . crowded with patrons who wear leather jackets, make a show of masculinity and scorn effeminate members of their world."

In response to ongoing raids by police, some of the city's bar owners formed the Tavern Guild in 1962, the first gay business association in the United States. It defended the rights of its members, their employees and patrons, retained legal assistance for anyone arrested near a gay bar, and raised money for homophile organizations. Among its many activities, it sponsored an annual picnic (above) and the annual Beaux Arts Ball (right), first held in 1963, an elegant affair to which guests arrived in everything from to limousines to low-cut gowns.

Cecil William, Ted McIlvenna, Robert Cromey, Chuck Lewis, and other ministers created the Council on Religion and the Homosexual (CRH) in 1964 to create better understanding between mainstream churches and homophile groups in San Francisco. As a fund-raiser, the council sponsored a costume ball on New Year's Day in 1965 at California Hall. Even with all permits secured, 35 uniformed and 15 plainclothes police showed up, photographing everyone entering the building and arresting several CRH attorneys, who protested their intimidation tactics. The next day, ministers associated with CRH held a news conference denouncing the police for "deliberate harassment and bad faith," making the general public well aware of the situation. When local media also condemned the police action, the department temporarily halted its raids on gay bars and appointed a member of the police community relations board to serve as a liaison to the gay community. At their trial two months later, the judge threw out the case against those arrested.

In 1965, when José Sarria (seated) was crowned Queen of the Beaux Arts Ball, he responded that because he already was a queen, he should be an empress instead. He took the name "Her Royal Majesty, José I, Empress of San Francisco, the Widow Norton," honoring 19th-century merchant and first emperor of the United States, Norton I. Thus the imperial court system, now an international organization, raises funds for many charities.

Some people publicly protested their treatment as gays. On Armed Forces Day, May 21, 1966, they held a rally on the steps of the federal building in San Francisco's Civic Center to protest their exclusion from the military. At a time when people could be denied employment or fired for their sexual orientation, it was in itself a public act of bravery.

A successor to the LCE, the Society for Individual Rights (SIR) soon became America's largest homophile organization. At the inaugural ceremonies for its community center in 1966, James Doran, SIR vice president, and a San Francisco police representative agreed on the need for good community relations with the department. The same year, the city hosted the National Planning Conference of Homophile Organizations, the first countrywide convention of lesbian and gay groups.

In August 1966, Compton's Cafeteria in the Tenderloin became a battleground between gays and police when police tried to evict a group of noisy customers, many who were drag queens. One officer received a cup of coffee in his face; the rest were routed by flying dishes, trays, and flatware. Not only was it a bumpy night, it was the first time gays forcibly resisted their oppression in the United States.

Maud's Study, the world's longest surviving lesbian bar, opened in the Haight in 1966. At the time, California law forbade women from being bartenders, so the honors in the early years went to men from nearby gay establishments.

By the time FeBe's opened in 1966, Folsom Street was well on its way to becoming leather's "Miracle Mile." Created by Mike Caffee, the bar's trademark, Michelangelo's David in leather pants, motorcycle jacket, and cap, became iconic. Closed briefly in 1970 when reports reached officials that patrons were using the back room for intimate socializing, the bar shut down for good in 1986.

Besides Febe's, the most popular establishments South of Market, also known as SoMa and SM, included the Ramrod (above), the Stud, and the Gas Station. At one time or another, the area also was home to the Covered Wagon, the Leatherneck, Dirty Sally's, the Plunge, the Eagle (below), and many others.

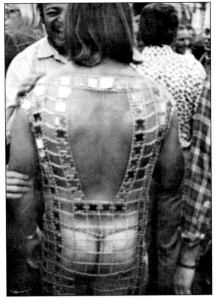

As the leather community became more organized, it began sponsoring events, first for itself, then for itself and the interested public. The California Motorcycle Club, founded in the 1960s, began hosting a carnival that attracted attendees from across the gay community. Attendees at the 1971 event, left, crowded the hall. One visitor to the 1972 carnival gave a new meaning to chain male.

By 1967, showing a growing awareness of the gay and lesbian community, some local politicians began attending "Candidates Nights" sponsored by SIR and the Daughters of Bilitis. Running for supervisor, future mayor and California senator Dianne Feinstein first met with potential lesbian and gay voters at one such meeting in 1969. The Alice B. Toklas Democratic Club emerged from SIR's political committee in 1972.

April 5, 1969   JUSTICE WEEKLY   Page Eleven

California Legislator Would Legalize Homo Acts Between "Consenting Adults"

San Francisco District Has More Sex Deviates Than Anywhere In State

It looks like Assemblyman Willie L. Brown, Jr., is trying to steal a leaf from Prime Minister Trudeau's "homosexual book" as the American, who claims his San Francisco district has more homosexuals than any other in California, has introduced a bill in Sacramento to legalize certain private sexual conduct between consenting adults. It is remembered that the Canadian Parliament is currently considering a similar piece of legislation as the result of the P.M. pointing out that the state has no right to be in the private bedroom of a Canadian.

In outlining his reasons for the bill, the legislator explained that similar ones have been adopted in the United Kingdom and Illinois—overlooking the impending Canadian measure — but he admitted the bill might have a tough time in California.

Pointed out the assemblyman: "What I'm attempting to do is knock out the blackmail and the public condemnation and free the police from being 'Peeping Toms' in restrooms so they can go out and do some honest criminal investigation."

the Democratic legislator, "I really don't expect any honest opposition, people have philosophical differences. I think there will be considerable practical political opposition based on people's feelings towards homosexuals."

Mr. Brown said the public "tend to discriminate" against
(Continued on Page 14)

Home Secretary Announces Loss Of Freedom Payment To Man Wrongly Detained

An ex-gratia payment from public funds of a yet-to-be-determined amount will be made to Ronald Avard, who was wrongly detained for three and a half years at Rampton Mental Hospital, it was announced by Britain's Home Secretary. Avard had been sent to the hospital after being found unfit to plead on two charges of sexual assault and attempted rape.

The 26-year-old man, who is said to have the mental age of a child of seven, was released and given an absolute discharge on the offences with which he was wrongly charged in July of 1965. He had signed a statement admitting the offences.

However, an investigation instituted by William Price, Labour M.P., disclosed that Avard had nothing to do with the incidents. However, it was not decided to lay charges against anybody else.

In a letter sent to Mr. Price — another was sent to Avard's father — it said the Home Secretary shared his view that "whatever the reasons which led to this unhappy situation, it calls for something more than the sympathy which we are all bound to feel for Mr. Avard and his family."

The letter to Mr. Price came from Mr. Elystan Morgan, Parliamentary Secretary at the Home Office.

Sex In Prison Finds Another Champion: Philadelphia Common Pleas Court Judge

Following the example of a Canadian M.P., a Phila-   He added that sex in the

The first attempt to change the legal restrictions against gays in California came in 1968, when San Francisco assemblyman Willie Brown introduced AB-743 to make sex between consenting adults legal. Assemblyman John Burton, also from San Francisco, cosponsored the bill. The legislation finally passed in 1975. Burton won a seat in the United States Congress in 1974, and Brown was elected San Francisco's mayor in 1994.

Postwar homophile organizations generally favored achieving greater civil rights through cooperation and understanding, but in the 1960s, more radical groups emerged that preferred activism and protest. In 1969, when someone dumped printers' ink onto demonstrators at the *San Francisco Examiner*, they used it to stamp their handprints onto the building. "The Night of the Purple Hand" became one of the decade's most visible protests against homophobia.

By 1971, when the Boot Camp opened, news of the leather community was appearing in Herb Caen's column in the *San Francisco Chronicle*. That year, the police stopped raiding gay bars in the city.

Wed., Aug 11, 1971 San Francisco Chronicle

HERB CAEN

BAY CITY BEAT: Well, duckies, you probably missed another fashionable social event — the grand opening of the Boot Camp, newest saloon along the city's flourishing sado-masochist strip (it's on Bryant, not too far from the Hall of Justice). Cristal, the Empress of S.F., was there, and so was the Dowager Empress, Jose, and all the leather motorcycle clubs for miles around. Mr. Dana won the Hunky Guy Contest (eat your hearts out) . . .

boot camp
1010 bryant
SAN FRANCISCO

*And visit THE CELL BLOCK
in our back room;
Custom Leather Gear
(Two blocks off Folsom)

San Francisco
THE MIRACLE MILE & SOUTH OF MARKET

In only 10 years, San Francisco had gone from having no leather bars at all to being home to a world-famous leather community with bars, baths, restaurants, hotels, and shops, all found on or near Folsom Street, "The Miracle Mile."

During the 1970s, Castro Street at the upper end of Market Street joined SoMa's "Miracle Mile" as a neighborhood with a concentration of gay businesses. The earliest establishments were bars and clubs, but as the area became a gay enclave, they soon were joined by bookstores, gift shops, clothiers, florists, coffee shops, and other businesses that opened specifically for a gay clientele.

Five

A COMMUNITY
OF COMMUNITIES

By 1970, San Francisco's reputation as the "homosexual capital of the United States" was secure. A grand exposé, *The Male Hustler*, published in 1966, stated, "One of the largest collections of members of the 'queer world' can be found in San Francisco. The Northern California metropolis is a virtual hotbed of perverts." *Knight: The Magazine for the Adult Male* described it in 1969 as "the most brazen, organized homosexual community in America," primarily because "this is a city that believes in tolerance for minority groups, and the homosexuals have found friends in the straight world to back up their own gay organizations." It estimated that close to 10 percent of the city's population, almost 90,000 people, was homosexual and that "homosexual establishments amount to 8%" of the total number of bars in the city. Any remaining challenge to the city's title vanished in 1972 when *That Certain Summer*, ABC's breakthrough Movie of the Week about average gays in love, was set, of course, in San Francisco.

Large numbers of lesbians and gays were able to patronize businesses of all kinds, from tourist meccas like Finocchio's to neighborhood taverns, leather bars, cocktail lounges, sweater bars, restaurants, magazine stands, shops, and bath houses. Not concentrated in a single neighborhood, they were found in North Beach, South of Market, Haight-Ashbury, the Tenderloin, Polk Street, and the Castro. Most of the places were for men—never more than 3 or 4 women's bars when there were more than 100 bars for men—but by the end of the decade, women, too, would have their own "downtown."

In the early 1970s, the famed Institute for Sex Research, founded by Alfred Kinsey, published a report, stating, "San Francisco is generally considered the best city in the United States for homosexuals." It was partly due to the city's "tradition of tolerance." Another factor was the city's size and geography, as it is smaller and less residentially dispersed than New York or Los Angeles, which made it "more conducive to a tightly knit homosexual community." One more reason was that local ownership and operation of lesbian and gay bars, clubs, and restaurants meant that proprietors had an interest in the community, not just their businesses, and a willingness to defend the rights of their patrons.

Because of groups like the Mattachine Society, the Society for Individual Rights, and the Tavern Guild, the report argued that "the San Francisco homosexual is well represented by a variety of organizations that attempt to make life easier for him." It concluded, "San Francisco meets the needs of its homosexual citizens better than any other place in this country." At the time, only two organizations in the United States were brave enough to have "homosexual" in their names.

Sexual behavior of gay San Franciscans was regulated by state law and enforced by observation, decoys, and entrapment. The California Penal Code made sodomy, the "infamous crime against nature," a felony, punishable by one year to life in prison, and it outlawed oral copulation, a felony for which the convicted could receive up to 15 years. Anyone convicted under these statutes had to register within 30 days with the chief of police or sheriff where he lived. It also made "disorderly conduct" a misdemeanor, a catchall that was the one most frequently used for punishing gays.

The next decade brought unimaginable change. Not only would San Franciscans be instrumental in repealing those sections of the penal code, but they would elect the country's first openly gay public official and establish lesbian and gay bands, choruses, sports leagues, and other social, cultural, and educational institutions.

Polk Street, on the western edge of the Tenderloin, became the city's first "gay downtown," with clubs, restaurants, retail shops, and hotels catering to lesbians and gays. The street's inaugural gay bar was the Nob Hill Club, which opened in 1950. It was raided and closed in 1959.

In its time, Buzzby's, which opened in 1974, probably was the most popular gay bar on Polk Street, also known affectionately as Polk Gulch or Polk Strasse. Decorated in high art deco, patrons might wait hours to get in the establishment. It closed in 1986.

The community staged its first pride parade on Saturday, June 27, 1970, when 30 or so "hair fairies" marched down Polk Street from Aquatic Park to city hall and rallied for "Christopher Street Liberation Day." Sunday's Gay-In, held at Speedway Meadows in Golden Gate Park (right), attracted considerably more participants. There was no organized pride celebration in 1971, but some 3,000 people participated in 1972's parade, also down Polk Street, and the number grew every year. Each march had a different theme—in 1974 (below), it was "Gay Freedom by '76." By the time the route changed to Market Street in 1976, the parade was attracting more than 200,000 participants and onlookers.

The community's celebration of Halloween began in North Beach but moved to Polk Street in the mid-1960s. When these revelers were photographed there in the mid-1970s, its center was moving once again, this time to the Castro, where it has been ever since. Once a spontaneous street party, it is now a major revelry on San Francisco's crowded social calendar.

Before it became a gay neighborhood, Eureka Valley was known to the world primarily for "the small cottage on Castro Street" that was the home of the Hanson family at the beginning of the 20th century. Kathryn Forbes told the Hanson family's story in the book *Mama's Bank Account*, published in 1943, and it was shared again in the play (Marlon Brando's Broadway debut as Nels), film, and television series (with Dick Van Patten as Nels) *I Remember Mama*.

Once a worker's neighborhood, its Victorians spared not only from the great earthquake and fire of 1906 but also from urban renewal in the 1950s and 1960s, Eureka Valley underwent dramatic change after World War II as the old residents moved to the suburbs and a new generation, including many lesbians and gays, moved in.

Eureka Valley's first gay bar, the Missouri Mule, opened in 1963. By the time it closed 10 years later, almost 30 others had come and gone in the neighborhood now known as the Castro. The site next became home to the Hombre, then Chops, Patsy's, and the Detour.

During the 1970s, the Castro, unlike anyplace else on earth, became a true gay men's town, a place where it was possible to live, work, shop, and socialize without ever interacting with straight people. Many saw the neighborhood as narrow and unwelcoming to women and minorities, but it showed what was possible when people were left alone to build a community.

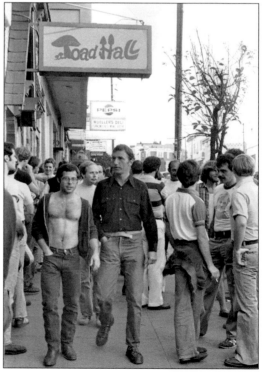

Toad Hall was Castro Street's gay hippie bar. Named for the lead character's home in *The Wind in the Willows*—one of the few children's classics with a gay subtext—and a nod toward a popular edible, it burned three times in 1973. Next it was, appropriately, the Phoenix. In 1997, the space became part of the pharmacy located next door.

The Twin Peaks opened in the 1940s as a neighborhood tavern. It became a gay bar when new owners bought it in 1972. Symbols of gay and lesbian progress, its large plate-glass windows were the first in an establishment whose customers in previous years typically had desired anonymity and privacy from passersby.

A growing sense of community and pride propelled the first annual Great Tricycle Race, which took place in 1972. Two-person crews, some in costume, rode, pushed, or carried their three-wheelers along a course that passed many of the city's gay watering holes. Entrants checked in at each location, often pausing for a libation as well. A Memorial Day tradition for 21 years, it raised money for numerous charities.

San Francisco's gay softball league, the first in the country, began informally in 1973 when eight local bars each sponsored a team. When other communities also formed associations, a gay world series became inevitable. The first was held in the city in October 1977, when New York's top team, the Ramrod, played the local champions, the Badlands, who won. The Community Softball League celebrated its 30th anniversary in 2003.

When Maud's won the first place championship in the Bay Area Women's Softball League in 1976, bar owner Rikki Streicher, front row center, posed with team members and their trophy. Other women's athletic competitions included basketball, bowling, football, ping-pong, and pool.

Lavender U was started in 1974 to provide "courses and interest groups for gay women and gay men." Offerings ranged from beginning and intermediate ballet to writing and answering personal ads, juggling as fun and therapy, communications skills, Greek cuisine, jewelry making, and workshops specifically for gay students, gay couples, gays over 40, and lesbian youth.

Among its many other visible achievements, the community created and exported the "Castro Clone" look, which became extremely popular—tennis shoes or boots, snug 501s, T-shirt, hooded jogging jacket (affectionately known as a "fag wrap"), short hair, and moustache. When some men started dying their jeans black, Levi Strauss began manufacturing them in that color, creating a mainstream style.

Harvey Milk organized the first Castro Street Fair in 1974 to show the Eureka Valley Merchants Association, then refusing to cooperate with the neighborhood's gay businessmen and women, the extent of the gay community. Once not much more than a wonderful Sunday afternoon block

party, the event grew into a major celebration of community pride that is attended by individuals and families from all over the Bay Area.

From the beginning, the Castro Street Fair included community organizations sharing information, artisans selling merchandise, and participants simply spending time in the sunshine—the most popular attractions have always been people watching and watching the unusual. At one early fair, a voter registration booth in front of Harvey Milk's camera shop (below) insured that lesbians and gays would be registered for the next election.

During the 1970s, the No. 8 bus, operating from the Embarcadero up Market Street to the Castro, took residents of the neighborhood to and from their jobs in the Civic Center, Union Square, and the Financial District. Known as "The Queen's Coach," pictured here at rest at Eighteenth and Castro Streets, it wore special livery for the American Bicentennial. At the end of the decade, a new underground station went in near the intersection of Market, Castro, and Seventeenth Streets, obliterating the former entrance to the Twin Peaks Tunnel. Just before it began running its new light railcars, engineers tested the system with their old rolling stock.

After a six-year struggle, California repealed its anti-sodomy law in 1975. When the state senate deadlocked on the legislation, Senate majority leader George Moscone locked the chamber doors until Lt. Gov. Milton Dymally could return from a trip to cast the tie-breaking vote. Gov. Jerry Brown signed the bill soon after. Elected mayor that November, Moscone and his wife celebrated at campaign headquarters.

Time featured San Franciscan Leonard Matlovich, center, on its cover in 1975 with the headline, "I am a homosexual: the gay drive for acceptance." At the time, the former air force sergeant was fighting to be reinstated in the armed forces, a first. He eventually lost the case, but his challenge of discrimination made him a gay public figure and role model for others.

Jo Daly (center) became the city's, and probably the nation's, first full-time paid liaison to the lesbian and gay community in 1975. When she told board of supervisors president Dianne Feinstein (behind her in doorway) that she and Nancy Achilles (hugging her) had decided to wed, the future United States senator invited them to use her home, where she performed the service herself, the only one present not wearing slacks.

By 1976, the San Francisco Gay Freedom Day Parade had become the largest such event in nation and largest parade in the city. That year saw several firsts: the first time the parade was on Market Street; the first time it received a mayoral proclamation, signed by recently elected George Moscone; and the first time (of only two) that the day's temperature reached more than 90 degrees.

From the beginning, the parade has been open to everyone who wished to participate: political clubs, community associations, professional societies, musical troupes, religious congregations, businesses and nonprofits, social groups, concerned individuals, and joyous, happy people. Over the years, many different organizations have joined the procession.

Dykes on Bikes began with a small contingent of women riders in the 1976 San Francisco Pride Parade. Now named the Women's Motorcycle Contingent, Dykes on Bikes, it continues to be inclusive of all women who ride motorcycles and wish to participate in the parade, where the group honors a long-established tradition of inaugurating the procession each year.

There had been gay bathhouses in San Francisco since the 1930s, but the Ritch Street Health Club not only advertised on a billboard at a major city intersection—Market, Castro, and Seventeenth Streets—it showed patrons using the facilities. Later the Bulldog Baths went one better, putting placards on the sides of Market Street buses.

With a growing awareness of its cultural contributions to the arts, the community held the world's first gay film festival in 1977. Now known as the San Francisco International LGBT Film Festival, the longest-running and largest LGBT arts event in North America, it has been joined by the Black GLBT Film Festival and the South Asian LGBT International Film Festival.

Theatre Rhinoceros was founded in 1977 to not only commission, foster, and present work by lesbian and gay artists but to explore and document the depth and breadth of the queer experience. One of best known and most successful gay theater companies in the world, it has presented everything from *Twelfth Night* to *Boys in the Band* to *Drag Queens from Outer Space*.

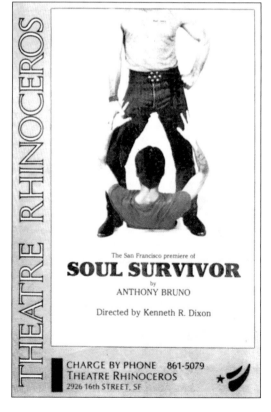

THEATRE RHINOCEROS

The San Francisco premiere of

SOUL SURVIVOR
by
ANTHONY BRUNO

Directed by Kenneth R. Dixon

CHARGE BY PHONE   861-5079
THEATRE RHINOCEROS
2926 16th STREET, SF

The gains made by the lesbian and gay community in individual rights were unpopular with political and religious extremists, who began to campaign for suppression. In 1977, the misguided movement found a spokesperson in Anita Bryant. "If gays are granted rights," she said, "next we'll have to give rights to prostitutes and to people who sleep with St. Bernards and to nailbiters."

Bryant's screed against gays led directly to the murder of Robert Hillsborough, a Golden Gate Park gardener. On the night of June 21, 1977, four youths screaming, "Faggot, faggot, faggot" and "This one's for Anita!" attacked and mortally wounded him. Mayor Moscone ordered flags flown at half-mast. As the Gay Freedom Day Parade passed city hall that year, many marchers placed flowers and signs there, creating a spontaneous memorial.

Traditionally a joyous celebration, the 1977 parade took notice of the threats to the community. Its most dramatic entry was "Bigots on Parade," created by Larry Agriesti. Marchers carried a poster-size photograph of Bryant flanked by pictures of Stalin, Hitler, the KKK, and Idi Amin. The simple and powerful statement later won a prestigious Cable Car award.

By the time Alfie's opened in the Castro in 1977, disco was the latest addition to the community's nightlife. Oil Can Harry's in the Tenderloin, the I-Beam in the Haight-Ashbury, Studio West near the Embarcadero, Trocodero Transfer in SoMa, and Different Strokes near Polk Street, among others, all became hugely popular.

More than anyone else, two people personified disco in the gay community—Sylvester, entertaining here at the Castro Street Fair, and Patrick Crowley, his frequent collaborator, whose own hits included "Megatron Man" and "Menergy," a celebration of the gay club sex scene. Sylvester's first solo album appeared in 1977. His second, 1978's Step II, included his first two disco classics, "You Make Me Feel (Mighty Real)," and "Dance (Disco Heat)."

In 1977, a wealthy Philadelphian bought Murphy's Resort, built in 1905 in Guenenville, and turned it into Fife's, a complete resort for gay men and women. Successful from opening day, other inns, lodges, bars, restaurants, dance clubs, and shops followed. For the next two decades, the Russian River became Northern California's answer to Fire Island, Provincetown, and Key West.

After two unsuccessful bids, Harvey Milk, by then "The Mayor of Castro Street," won election to the San Francisco Board of Supervisors on November 8, 1977, the city's first openly gay elected official. On his first day in office the following January, he walked to work from the Castro down Market Street to city hall, joined by thousands of supporters who visibly showed the community's increasing political power.

So deeply did the new supervisor believe in freedom and equality that he took every opportunity to condemn hate and bigotry and to march in protest against anti-gay initiatives and ballot measures, including a demonstration, seen here, against a Miami ballot initiative to repeal that city's gay rights ordinance.

Milk soon made a difference in human rights, introducing legislation that barred the city from doing business with contractors and organizations that discriminated against lesbians and gays. Mayor Moscone quickly signed the new ordinance.

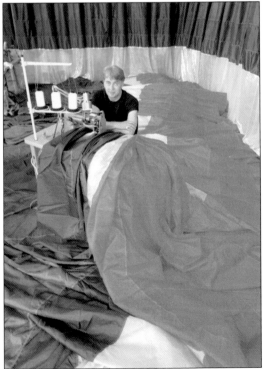

The rainbow flag debuted at the Gay Freedom Day Parade in 1978. The six stripes represent the following: red for life, orange for healing, yellow for sun, green for serenity with nature, indigo for harmony, and violet for spirit. Designed by Gilbert Baker, it became an international symbol of lesbian and gay pride. For its 25th anniversary, its creator posed with and within his creation.

The San Francisco Gay Freedom Day Marching Band and Twirling Corps (now the San Francisco Gay/Lesbian Freedom Band) debuted at the 1978 pride parade, the first musical organization in the world to include "lesbian" or "gay" in its name.

NEVER AGAIN!

FIGHT ▼ BACK!

The pink triangle was used to identify the thousands of gay people who died in concentration camps in Nazi German

The lesbian and gay community barely had time to celebrate its political and social gains before the political extremists turned from words to actions with Proposition 6 in 1978. If passed, the ballot initiative would have expelled from the school system all homosexual teachers and all heterosexual teachers who might present homosexuality positively. At first leading in the polls, the measure lost 2-1 in the state and 3-1 in San Francisco.

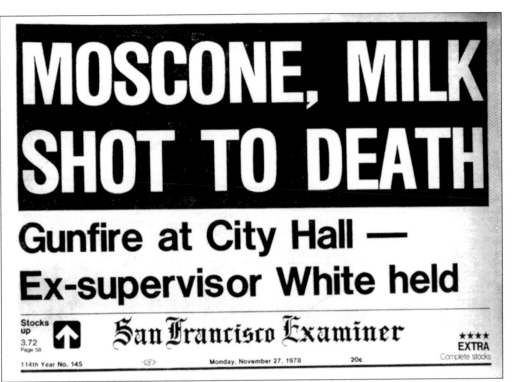

MOSCONE, MILK SHOT TO DEATH

Gunfire at City Hall — Ex-supervisor White held

Stocks up 3.72 Page 58

San Francisco Examiner

★★★★ EXTRA
Complete stocks

114th Year No. 145　　Monday, November 27, 1978　　20¢

On November 27, 1978, barely three weeks after the defeat of Proposition 6, Supervisor Milk and Mayor Moscone were assassinated in their city hall offices by Dan White, a former supervisor.

That evening, a candlelight march of 30,000 mourners retraced Harvey Milk's walk from the Castro to the Civic Center on his first day in office only 11 months earlier. The San Francisco Gay Men's Chorus, the first men's chorus to have the word "gay" in its name, began that night on the steps of city hall, singing to comfort the grieving.

Although Dan White had brought a loaded gun to city hall, shot Mayor Moscone four times, reloaded, shot Supervisor Milk five times, went to church for absolution, turned himself in, and confessed, a jury found him guilty only of two counts of voluntary manslaughter on May 21, 1979. That evening, members of the community protested at city hall, breaking windows and burning police cars. Later police retaliated, smashing up the Elephant Walk at Eighteenth and Castro Streets.

Gay Run '80, the first gay-organized footrace sanctioned by the Amateur Athletic Union, attracted runners from 10 states, ages 15 to 63. At a time of continuing governmental and fundamentalist attempts to marginalize the community, it provided "another way for gay people to express and feel good about themselves." The same year, both Bay Area Career Women and Black and White Men Together were founded in San Francisco.

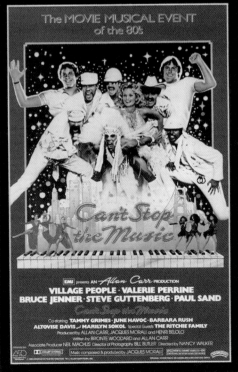

Although no one knew it then, the Village People's 1980 appearance in San Francisco to film the conclusion of their film, *Can't Stop the Music*, marked not only the end of disco—some credited the film itself with that—but the end of an era for gays everywhere. The next year, the *New York Times* ran an article titled, "Rare Cancer Seen in 41 Homosexuals," signaling the age of AIDS.

AMERICAN INDIAN AIDS INSTITUTE OF SAN FRANCISCO

ASIANS & AIDS:
WHAT'S THE CONNECTION?

Asian AIDS PROJECT

2024 Hayes Street
San Francisco, CA 94117
415/929-1304

A project of Asian American
Recovery Services, Inc.

Illustrations courtesy of Douglas Simonson. For further information,
write 4614 Kilauea Avenue, #330, Honolulu, HI 96816, or call
808/737-6275. Artwork © 1988 Douglas Simonson. All rights
reserved.

This material is produced with funding from the AIDS Clearance Fund.

Design: Kent Teyendaks

Black People Get AIDS Too.

Call the S.F. Black Coalition on AIDS Help-Line: (415) 346-AIDS

HABLEMOS.

CHARLAS
INFORMALES PARA
HOMBRES GAY

TODOS LOS
JUEVES A LAS
7:00 PM

PARA MAYOR INFORMACION
LLAMAR A JUAN RODRIGUEZ
EDUCADOR DE LA SALUD.
TELEFONO:

415-647-5450

LATINO AIDS PROJECT

LET'S TALK.

DROP-IN GROUP
FOR LATINO
GAY MEN

EVERY
THURSDAY
AT 7:00 PM

FOR DETAILED INFORMATION
CALL: JUAN RODRIGUEZ
HEALTH EDUCATION
PHONE NUMBER:

415-847-5450

LATINO AIDS PROJECT

Lesbians and AIDS
What's the Connection?

The tragedy and reality of AIDS united the different people who make up San Francisco's lesbian and gay community like no other development or dilemma. Realizing the importance of everyone getting vital information and services as quickly as possible and in a way that would be useful to them, numerous organizations published pamphlets, established hot lines, held meetings, and offered assistance that not only helped people but also recognized and respected their ethnic and cultural sensitivities. The illustration on the cover of the American Indian AIDS Institute brochure was by Harry Fonseca. A drawing by Douglas Simonson graced "Asians & AIDS" for the Asian AIDS Project. Renown Bay Area photographer Cathy Cade created the image for "Lesbians and AIDS," produced by the Women's AIDS Project.

Six

SORROW AND SOLIDARITY

By the beginning of the 1980s, lesbians and gays had created several vital and vibrant communities in San Francisco, but the Castro had emerged not only as the largest gay neighborhood in the city—and the one with highest per capita gay population in the world—but as the center of local gay politics. Its popularity among men especially put tremendous pressure on housing costs, tripling the rent of a three-bedroom flat from $245 a month in 1975 to $750 a month just five years later.

Because women typically made less money for the same work than men, and had fewer opportunities for advancement to higher paying jobs, gay men could pay more for housing. Increased housing costs thus forced many lesbians out of the Castro. Those who did not leave the city altogether created new neighborhoods for themselves on Potrero Hill, Bernal Heights, and along Valencia Street.

Lesbians and gays created more than just neighborhoods. They had established social, cultural, religious, and service institutions—dance troupes, newspapers, choirs, magazines, theater companies, film festivals, churches and synagogues, bookstores, gift stores, restaurants, and clubs—that contributed to the enrichment and joy of daily life. They organized against discrimination and fought back political attacks. If they had not yet achieved equal rights, at least they had achieved political strength and vitality.

Then the impossible, the unthinkable, the unimaginable happened. The community became victim to the most devastating human plague since the Middle Ages.

No one knows when the virus that became known as HIV first infected San Franciscans (it was present in blood samples taken for hepatitis studies in the 1970s and retested many years later), but in early 1981 rumors of a "gay cancer" began circulating in the community. By the time the disease, first called Gay-related Immune Deficiency (GRID), received the name Acquired Immune Deficiency Syndrome (AIDS) in 1982, many were dying in the city and elsewhere and more were getting sick. What made matters exasperating were that no cause had been identified and no known treatment could help. The best of times had become the worst of times.

Not until January 1983 did researchers at the Pasteur Institute in Paris isolate what they believe was the virus that caused the disease. It took another two years for the United States Food and Drug Administration to license the first test to detect the virus's antibodies in human blood and two years more for the agency to approve AZT for use as the first anti-AIDS drug. By then, physicians and health departments in the United States reported that more than 23,000 Americans had died from the disease. Because of government inaction, the number of AIDS deaths by the end of 2005 was greater than 530,000, including more than 18,000 San Franciscans.

Despite causing devastation beyond comprehension to the entire community, lesbians and gays from all backgrounds began to create the services victims needed when no private organizations or public agencies were willing to help. Remarkably they also continued their fight to gain the "certain unalienable Rights . . . Life, Liberty, and the pursuit of Happiness" to which all people "are endowed by their Creator."

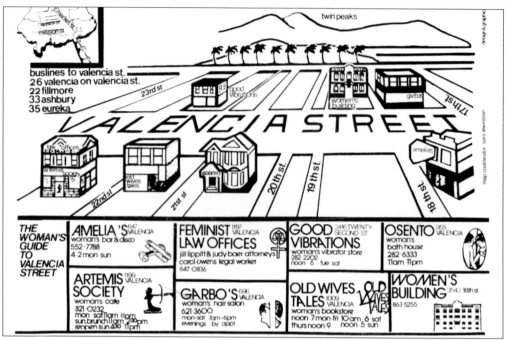

In the early 1980s, San Francisco evolved a fourth queer neighborhood, centered along what became known as the Valencia Corridor. Many of its establishments focused primarily on the needs of lesbians and bisexual women and included professional services, goods, and social space.

The Woman's Building opened to provide meeting space for women's organizations and learning programs. The first woman-owned and operated community center in the country, its *MaestraPeace* mural, painted in 1994 by seven women artists and their associates, covers two exterior walls with representations of the healing power of women's wisdom over time, women's contributions to humanity, and the making of history by women from all continents and cultures.

Located in a renovated mortuary, with the embalming room still intact, the Valencia Rose opened in 1980 as a center for gay and lesbian arts. It showcased a wide variety of performers, including (clockwise from far left) "queer comics" Jeanine Strobel, Lea DeLaria, Kelly Kittell, Tom Ammiano, "The Mother of Gay Comedy" Doug Holsclaw, Monica Palacios, Danny Williams, and Linda Moakes. The venue closed in 1986.

Most of the Valencia Rose comics continued in entertainment, but Tom Ammiano, who also taught elementary school, entered politics. The first gay public school teacher in San Francisco to publicly disclose his sexual orientation, he was elected to the city's board of education in 1990, an amazing achievement for an openly gay man in any city. He won a seat on the board of supervisors in 1994 and became board president in 1998.

When the community's Halloween celebration became centered in the Castro, it became a major social and cultural event. Every costume was valid, from Star Whores—R U 1 2, Princess Letus, and Hand Solo—to the Tutu Fabulous Ballet Corps, whose lovely ballerinas all sported clone moustaches.

Halloween also was observed on Folsom Street, where celebrants might be dressed as anything from satyrs to sailors, some in costumes worn only that night, and, one year at least, a pair of stiletto heels, which waited patiently for the next passerby.

The inspiration of the Sisters of Perpetual Indulgence, the first Castro Dog Show and Parade was held in 1981, where a wide variety of dogs and owners competed for prizes. Judges at the second annual event included Shirley MacLaine. Proceeds went to the newly formed Kaposi's Sarcoma Cancer Clinic. Responding to a "causes unknown" crisis, the Sisters also published one of the earliest sets of guidelines for safer sex.

Not until mid-1981 did anyone suspect AIDS existed. On June 5, the Centers for Disease Control reported five cases, without identifiable cause, of pneumocystis carinii pneumonia in five men, all active homosexuals. At first called GRID (Gay-related Immunodeficiency Disease), the term AIDS was adopted in 1982 when it became obvious that anyone could get the disease. Soon the best available information appeared in the lesbian and gay community.

111

In December 1981, Bobbi Campbell, also known as Sister Florence Nightmare, R.N., became the first San Franciscan to publicly disclose that he was a person with AIDS. As "AIDS Poster Boy," he appeared on the cover of *Newsweek*; helped found The Kaposi's Sarcoma Research and Education Foundation with Marcus Conant, M.D., Cleve Jones, and others; and with Dan Turner, organized People With AIDS San Francisco, the first organization of, for, and by people with AIDS.

San Franciscan Dr. Tom Waddell, a former Olympian, established the Gay Olympic Games to celebrate the accomplishments of lesbian and gay athletes. The U.S. Olympic Committee forced Waddell to delete "olympic" in the organization's name, although it allows frog, pancake, math, and urology olympics, among others. It then sued him for court costs totaling almost $100,000. The first two meets were held in San Francisco in 1982 and 1986. They have been held in different major cities around the world every four years since.

The first AIDS Candlelight March took place on May 2, 1983. Organized in San Francisco by Bobby Reynolds, Gary Walsh, and Bobbi Campbell, it marked the first time Persons With Aids (PWAs) marched behind a banner proclaiming what was to become the motto of the PWA self-empowerment movement: "FIGHTING FOR OUR LIVES."

FIGHTING FOR OUR LIVES

AN AIDS CANDLELIGHT MARCH
A personal expression to honor the dead and support the living.

SAN FRANCISCO
7:30 P.M.
FROM CASTRO & MARKET
TO U.N. PLAZA/CIVIC CENTER
BRING CANDLE
INFO / AIDS & KS FOUNDATION
(415) 864-4376

NEW YORK
8:00 P.M.
FROM SHERIDAN SQUARE
TO FEDERAL BUILDING
BRING CANDLE AND WEAR
BLACK ARMBAND WITH
PINK TRIANGLE
INFO / GMHC HOTLINE
(212) 685-4952

Organized by
NY AIDS Network **MONDAY, MAY 2, 1983**

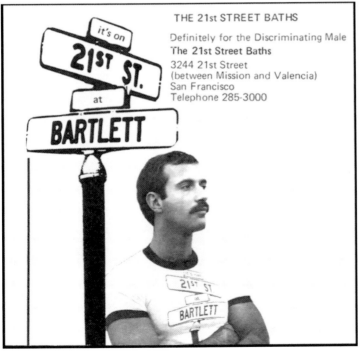

THE 21st STREET BATHS

Definitely for the Discriminating Male
The 21st Street Baths
3244 21st Street
(between Mission and Valencia)
San Francisco
Telephone 285-3000

it's on
21ST ST.
at
BARTLETT

In response to the crisis and under tremendous political pressure, the San Francisco Department of Public Health used its authority in 1984 to order all of the city's bathhouses to close. By then, business at many of the bathhouses was down by more than 50 percent. The 21st Street Baths, the city's last gay bathhouse, shut its doors in 1987.

113

The first Folsom Street Fair was held in 1984. More than simply a joyous celebration, it was organized by a group of community and housing activists to show that there was a viable neighborhood South of Market, one which was increasingly being threatened by urban redevelopment. The dominance of the leather community in the area turned the fair into the world's largest leather event, even after urban renewal vanquished the residents.

Up Your Alley, a second, smaller SoMa street fair for the leather community, started in 1985. First held in then notorious Ringold Alley, it relocated to then notorious Dore Alley in 1987. A single, nonprofit organization now produces both the Folsom Street and Dore Alley fairs, which raise money for numerous community services.

The National March for Lesbian and Gay Rights took place the day before the 1984 Democratic Convention, which was held in San Francisco for the first time since 1920. A major focus was protesting the lack of federal action to deal with AIDS. In front of the same convention, BiPOL sponsored the first Bisexual Rights Rally.

Because government was slow or failed to act, the community responded with what became known as the San Francisco Model, a safety net of mostly private organizations and volunteers that helped with the most vital daily needs of people with AIDS—food, shelter, quality of life, counseling, testing, legal assistance, and education. Among many groups providing vital assistance, the AIDS Emergency Fund (above) began in 1982 to help pay basic living costs such as rent, utility bills, and medical expenses for poverty-level San Franciscans with HIV or AIDS and to help clients avoid eviction or utility shutoff, improve the quality of their lives, and maintain stable housing. Founded by Ruth Brinker in 1985, Project Open Hand (below) provided meals, when no other social service agency did so, to those too weak or too impoverished from AIDS to feed themselves.

Recognizing the legacy also being lost with the loss of lives, a group of concerned residents founded the San Francisco Bay Area Gay and Lesbian Historical Society in 1985 to preserve local LGBT history. Now called the Gay Lesbian Bisexual Transgender Historical Society of Northern California, the organization maintains a museum, an archive, and a research center open to anyone who wishes to learn more about the city's queer past.

GLBT **HISTORICAL SOCIETY**
San Francisco, California

MUSEUM

Gallery & Exhibits

ARCHIVE

Internationally Renowned

Incredible collection of photos, flyers, posters, artifacts, memorabilia, ephemera & memoirs

Research Center

The ARC/AIDS vigil began on October 27, 1985, at the United Nations Plaza in San Francisco's Civic Center to bring attention to the connections between poverty, homelessness, and HIV. Members of the group also distributed health information and held marches, protests, and rallies to bring attention to the need for help for people with ARC and AIDS and to the slow or nonexistent response of government.

Cleve Jones established the Names Project and created the first quilt panel to remember his friend Marvin Feldman in 1986. With panels from every state and dozens of countries, it is now the largest community art project in the world, seen by more than 14 million people worldwide. In 1989, the quilt was nominated for a Nobel Peace Prize.

Impatient with government response to the AIDS epidemic, ACT-UP SF (AIDS Coalition To Unleash Power), formed out of the AIDS Action Coalition, turned to picketing, protest, sit-ins, lie-ins, confrontation, and civil disobedience—anything that would draw attention and assistance to the crisis. ACT-UP in turn gave birth to Queer Nation, which used the same strategies to bring public awareness and change to other lesbian and gay issues.

In 1988, a group of San Franciscans decided to create a living tribute in Golden Gate Park to those lost to AIDS. Five years after work on the site began in 1991, Congress passed the "National AIDS Memorial Grove Act," officially designating the park's historic DeLaveaga Dell as the nation's first AIDS memorial. Unlike most national memorials, however, it is not listed on the National Register of Historic Places.

Designed simply to save lives and prevent sadness, the San Francisco AIDS Foundation's "Life Liberty and the Pursuit of Happiness" campaign became controversial when some who figuratively drape themselves in the flag denounced a photograph showing two men draped in it literally, although they showed less skin than a bathing suit ad. This was one in a series of campaigns sponsored by the agency.

119

DOMESTIC PARTNERS

ON _____ 199 ___

NANCY ALFARO, COUNTY CLERK OF THE CITY AND COUNTY OF SAN FRANCISCO, CERTIFIES THAT

_____ *and*

_____

BECAME DOMESTIC PARTNERS BY FILING A DECLARATION OF DOMESTIC PARTNERSHIP IN THE OFFICE OF THE COUNTY CLERK.

NANCY ALFARO
COUNTY CLERK

BY _____

DEPUTY COUNTY CLERK

Established February 14, 1991 San Francisco Admin. Code Chapter 62
CITY AND COUNTY OF SAN FRANCISCO

San Francisco established its domestic partners registry through a referendum passed in 1990. On February 14, 1991, the day it became available, more than 275 lesbian and gay couples registered at city hall and domestic partner benefits became available to city and county employees. In 1997, companies having contracts with the city were required to offer the same benefits to their unmarried domestic partners as to their married employees.

San Francisco hosted its first Dyke March in 1992. Now attracting more than 50,000 women, it is the largest lesbian celebration in the world. Its objectives are to "fight for freedom, for power, for sisterhood, for love, for control of our bodies, for self defense, for dignity, for human rights, for our children, for joy, for liberation, for sex, for equality, for justice, for our lives, for all women forever!"

Opened in the city's new main library in 1996, the James C. Hormel Gay and Lesbian Center was the first in a public library in the United States dedicated to collecting, preserving, and studying lesbian, gay, bisexual, and transgender culture and achievement. The next year, San Francisco philanthropist Hormel himself made history when he became the first openly gay American to be nominated for an ambassadorship.

In 1998, two of those who hate assaulted and lynched Matthew Shepard, a 21-year-old University of Wyoming student, tying him to a fence and leaving him to die because he was gay. When news of the tragedy reached San Francisco, a spontaneous memorial emerged at Eighteenth and Castro Streets.

The San Francisco Lesbian Gay Bisexual Transgender Community Center opened in March 2002. The first center in the United States built from the ground up and among the largest in the world, it provides a broad range of legal, wellness, social, educational, and cultural programs and services to benefit LGBT people throughout their lives.

Stating, "Today a barrier to true justice has been removed," newly inaugurated mayor Gavin Newsom authorized same-sex marriages in San Francisco on February 12, 2004. Some believed that a presidential election year was not the right time to challenge discrimination, but others argued that there is no wrong moment to demand equality. As word spread, a line soon formed around city hall.

Because it was Abraham Lincoln's birthday, the great emancipator himself, sitting in his customary place outside city hall, expressed his approval with a sign that proclaimed, "We all deserve the freedom to marry."

The grandeur of city hall provided a perfect setting for the joyous and historic ceremonies that took place after applicants had filed their marriage licenses with the Office of the County Clerk. More than 80 couples were married the first day.

The first license issued and the first marriage performed was for pioneer activists Phyllis Lyon and Del Martin. Although they had been a couple for more than 50 years, an anniversary seldom reached in any relationship, no previous government had recognized the validity of their union. Assessor-recorder Mabel Teng conducted their service, after which Mayor Newsom himself congratulated the newlyweds.

Before the day ended, almost two dozen same-sex weddings were performed in city hall and officials issued some dozen more marriage licenses to lesbian and gay couples, their documents stating "spouse for life" instead of "husband and wife."

Except for a few venomous picketers, each newlywed leaving city hall was greeted with applause, flowers, best wishes, and love by those still waiting in line or simply observing the festivities. Before the California Supreme Court ordered San Francisco officials to cease issuing the licenses on March 11, 2004, more than 4,000 same-sex couples had applied for them.

Despite that setback, the 2004 and 2005 the Gay Lesbian Bisexual Transgender Parades that followed were joyous affairs, attended by an estimated one million people. Mayor Newsom not only proclaimed the parade each year, he marched the parade route, stopping to greet well-wishers all along the way.

As always, the participants represent and reflect the great diversity within the community.

Whatever the future, lesbian and gay San Franciscans rightfully are proud of the communities they have built, the successes they have achieved, and the contributions they have made to the culture, politics, and progress of the city, all intrinsically and integrally woven into the fabric of place and people that is San Francisco.

DISCOVER THOUSANDS OF LOCAL HISTORY BOOKS
FEATURING MILLIONS OF VINTAGE IMAGES

Arcadia Publishing, the leading local history publisher in the United States, is committed to making history accessible and meaningful through publishing books that celebrate and preserve the heritage of America's people and places.

Find more books like this at
www.arcadiapublishing.com

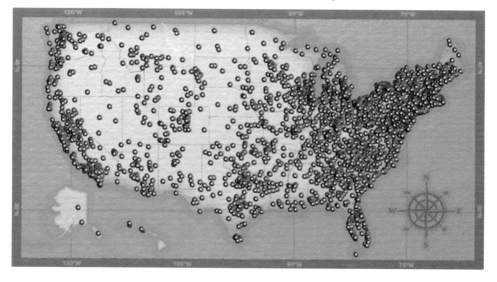

Search for your hometown history, your old stomping grounds, and even your favorite sports team.

Consistent with our mission to preserve history on a local level, this book was printed in South Carolina on American-made paper and manufactured entirely in the United States. Products carrying the accredited Forest Stewardship Council (FSC) label are printed on 100 percent FSC-certified paper.

MADE IN THE USA